Marketing Research

Marketing Engineering Applications

Gary L. Lilien
The Pennsylvania State University

Arvind Rangaswamy
The Pennsylvania State University

Co-sponsored by

**Institute for
the Study of
Business Markets**

ADDISON-WESLEY

An imprint of Addison Wesley Longman, Inc.

Reading, Massachusetts • Menlo Park, California • New York • Harlow, England
Don Mills, Ontario • Sydney • Mexico City • Madrid • Amsterdam

ISBN: 0-321-04647-1

12345678910-CRS-0201009998

CONTENTS

To my love and best friend,
Dorothy, for sharing her time
with one more book.
                            -Gary

To Ann for her love and support,
and Cara for providing the
needed distraction.
                            -Arvind

PREFACE

Rapid changes in the marketplace, in data, and in the computing environment are transforming the structure and content of the marketing manager's job. As a profession, marketing is evolving so that it is no longer based primarily on conceptual content. While many view traditional marketing as an art and some view it as a science, the new marketing increasingly looks like engineering (that is, combining art and science to solve specific problems).

There will always be a role for marketing concepts. Indeed, to make use of the powerful information tools now available requires sound conceptual grounding. But marketers need more than concepts to fully exploit the resources available to them. They need to move beyond conceptual marketing toward what we call marketing engineering: the use of interactive computer decision models to help support marketing decisions. While such needs are evident throughout the field of marketing, they are central to effective marketing research.

This package of materials is designed to supplement a course in Marketing Research. It includes selections from our book, *Marketing Engineering* (Addison Wesley Longman, 1998) that are appropriate for such courses. Those selections are designed to make the corresponding course material come alive with hands-on exercises and cases.

Although each piece of software included here has associated with it a corresponding case or problem, all of the software (except the Promotional Spending Analysis spreadsheet) is independent of those cases and can be used separately on other case-problems or on real problems. Two of the software programs—TreeÅge and ScanUS—are supplied as student versions of commercial packages, whereas we developed the other five pieces of software.

We have selected seven tools and applications that have broad relevance in marketing research courses:

1. **Needs-based Segmentation Using Cluster Analysis**: This general software tool performs cluster analysis, factor analysis and discriminant analysis. The accompanying case addresses how to segment the market on the basis of needs for a sample of prospective buyers for a new personal digital assistant. The case raises issues such as: (1) How many segments should the firm consider (and how do those segments differ)? (2) Which of those segments should the firm target? (3) How many different products should the firms offer? (4) How should the new product be positioned? (See Positioning Analysis, below.)

2. **Targeting: Using Regression and Multinomial Logit Analysis:** This software tool allows the user to apply both regression and logit analysis to a customer targeting application: developing a direct mail campaign that targets the best/most responsive customers. In

its application to the Bookbinders' Book Club case, it allows the student to compare a "judgmental" targeting approach with the results of a regression based as well as a logit-model approach.

3. **Product Positioning Using Perceptual Mapping**: This software tool takes customer perceptions and preferences for products and produces a two or three dimensional map that allows the user to view alternative product positions and consider the strategic implications of changes in that positioning. The accompanying case looks at positioning the Infiniti G20 in 1990: given customer perceptions and preferences for new cars in 1990, how should Infiniti position this car in the market. (We also include a data set that is related to the PDA segmentation case.)

4. **Product Design Using Conjoint Analysis**: This software implements the full-profile version of conjoint analysis. The program allows users to: (1) Construct the conjoint design by specifying new product attributes and options. (2) Obtain data from customers for the chosen design. (3) Conduct market simulations using data from customers to determine the product design(s) that will generate the highest market share(s). We include a hotel design exercise for forte Hotels to illustrate the use of conjoint analysis.

5. **Making Decisions Under Uncertainty Using Decision Trees (TreeÅge)**: The software permits easy implementation of decision trees to isolate the factors that have the most influence on decisions that have uncertain consequences. The software also allows the student to determine the value of marketing research that may reduce the decision uncertainty. We include a case: ICI America's Product Selection case, where the concepts and tools can be applied.

6. **Retail Site Location Using Geodemographic Data and Models (ScanUs)**: Geodemographic data, in conjunction with a gravity model can be used to determine the relative attractiveness and market potential of different retail sites. The associated case—J&J Video Store location—illustrates how this important new data source and related computer tools can be used.

7. **Promotional Analysis Using Scanner Panel Data and Multinomial Logit Analysis**: Scanner panel data—an increasingly pervasive data source—can be used in conjunction with a modeling framework like logit analysis to evaluate promotional effectiveness and develop promotional plans for packaged goods. The associated case, MassMart Inc, demonstrates how these concepts and tools can be applied to improve the profitability of promotional plans.

The pedagogic philosophy here involves two main principles: learning by doing and end-user modeling. What this means is that the way you will learn these concepts best is to try to apply the software to the problem and make some specific recommendations based on your experience. Thus you learn the concept by doing it yourself—not merely by studying the concept or by assigning the analysis to some staff member or consultant.

This volume contains both software tutorials (step by step instructions on how to use the software) as well as the problem sets or cases that are keyed to the concept. *We strongly recommend that you go through each tutorial (making sure you can reproduce the results there) before attempting to "solve" the case.* Our experience is that well over 90% of the difficulties users have running the software are solved by simply reproducing the screens in the respective tutorial.

Also, read the first section of this tutorial carefully—it not only tells you how to install the software, but it provides a number of other general hints about using the software.

To get other software hints and updates, please visit our website: *http://hepg.awl.com/lilien-rangaswamy/mktgeng/.* You can also send us your comments and suggestions about the software by using the e-mail facility available at this site.

Acknowledgments

This book grew out of the multi-year effort that we have termed *Marketing Engineering* and represents an evolution of our vision to put marketing modeling concepts and tools into more general use. We gratefully acknowledge the support of the companies that sponsor Penn State's Institute for the Study of Business Markets, whose generous support made this entire effort possible. We also thank Mike Roche at Addison Wesley Longman and series editor Joel Steckel at New York University who helped us shape the final product.

While we wrote portions of the software, we were involved more in the design and testing of the actual implementation of the codes. Key software were implemented by Louis Jia, Animesh Karna, Jean-François Latour, John Lin, Andrew "Nuke" Stollak, and Jianan Wu. Our students, Lakshmi Anand, Tolga Gurkin, Katrin Starke, Selva Vaidiyanathan, and David Wu, provided additional, essential support.

The entire manuscript was produced by Mary Wyckoff. In addition to her manuscript preparation, Mary managed the entire process and kept us relaxed and cheerfully on schedule. We are deeply grateful for her dedication to this effort!

We also thank the many early adopters of *Marketing Engineering* whose unwavering support and gentle prods to correct software glitches have helped us to continuously improve this product. Thanks to all!

Gary L. Lilien
Arvind Rangaswamy
June 1998

INTRODUCTION

MARKETING RESEARCH SOFTWARE (VERSION 1.0)

Installing Marketing Research: Marketing Engineering Applications

Installing the software onto your computer's hard disk is an easy process, but you should still read through the entire installation instructions before you start.

A. This software is supplied to you on a CD-ROM. Before you start, make sure that you have the proper hardware and operating system:

Minimum configuration: IBM-compatible PCs running the 486 processor (33 MHz), 16 MB RAM, 15 MB available hard disk space, and a CD-ROM drive.

Recommended configuration: IBM-compatible PCs running the Pentium or equivalent processor (133 MHz or better), 32MB RAM, 15 MB available hard disk space, and a CD-ROM drive.

Operating system: Windows 95 and Windows NT.

Microsoft Excel: Parts of this software require the availability of Microsoft Excel 7 or higher. If you have not installed Excel on your system, you may still be able to use the non-Excel models included in this package.

B. *Installing the software*

1. Start Windows.

2. Insert the Marketing Engineering CD-ROM into your CD-ROM drive.

3. Run the setup.exe application in drive x:\, where x is the letter of your CD-ROM drive.

4. Follow the instructions on the screen to complete the installation. We recommend that you install this program in the default directory C:\Program Files\MktgEng, although it will work on any non-network (local) drive.

C. *Uninstalling the software*

1. Start Windows.

2. Open **Control Panel**.

3. Open **Add/Remove Programs**.

4. Select **Marketing Engineering**. Click **Add/Remove** button.

Required add-ins for running Excel applications

For Excel applications, you need the Solver tool. Solver is not part of the default configuration when you install Microsoft Excel. Under the **Tools** menu on your version of Excel, check the list of **Add-Ins** to see whether they are included. If not, run the Excel (or MS Office) setup procedure (with the original installation disks or CD) and select the appropriate options to install Solver.

Setting up Marketing Engineering after installation

Setting preferences: If you wish to customize the location of the files used by the program, go to the **Help** menu and select **Preferences**. In particular, make sure that the path to Excel.exe is correctly specified.

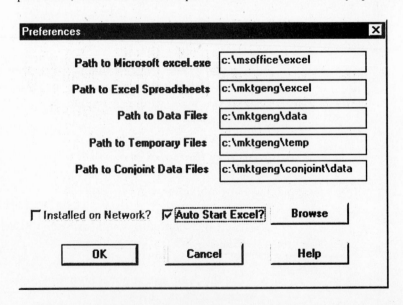

You can install the software on a network only with the network version of Marketing Engineering. If you check **Auto Start Excel,** the program will automatically start Excel every time you open Marketing Engineering. If you turn off this option, you can still open Excel whenever you want to by going to the **File** menu and choosing **Open Excel**.

Opening applications: When you start Marketing Engineering, you will briefly see the following screen:

On the **Model** menu select a model, e.g., **Positioning Analysis**.

NOTE: *Only models that appear as active menu items can be opened. The non-activated items are part of the full Marketing Engineering suite of programs.*

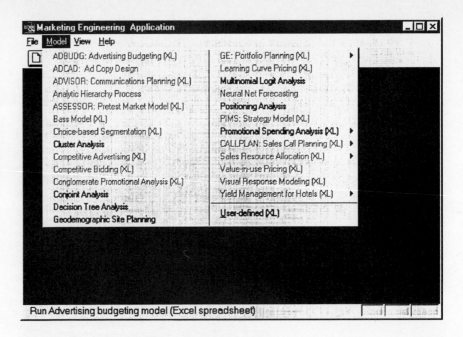

Tips for using the software

Marketing Engineering consists of three different types of software modules:

1. Windows-based programs that will run directly off the Marketing Engineering main menu:
    - Cluster Analysis
    - Multinomial Logit Analysis
    - Positioning Analysis

2. A spreadsheet model that will be loaded under Excel:
    - Promotional Spending Analysis

3. Stand-alone applications that are "loosely" connected to the main menu and are simply executed when invoked:
    - Conjoint Analysis
    - Decision Tree Analysis
    - Geodemographic Site Planning

   Select **Index** under the **Help** menu to get information about individual models and how to run them.

NOTE: *The following tips apply only to* **Microsoft Excel applications** *(Promotional Spending Analysis).*

Opening Excel models directly: You can open Excel models directly by clicking on *.xls files located in the (default) directory, C:\Program Files\MktgEng\Excel. This can be helpful if you have limited memory on your computer system to load the full Marketing Engineering program. If you move the Excel files to a new directory, make sure that the file modgen97.ind is also located in the new directory.

Moving between the main Marketing Engineering window and an Excel application: To move back and forth between the Marketing Engineering main window and an Excel application you can use the ALT+TAB key combination. You can also get back to the Marketing Engineering main window from an Excel application by going to the **Model** menu and clicking **Back to Mktg. Eng.**

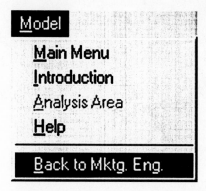

Entering data into a Excel spreadsheet: After you enter data in a cell, press the Enter key to ensure that the data gets registered within the spreadsheet.

Using Solver: In some cases the Solver runs in Excel will not converge. You may then have to provide Solver with new starting values. See Appendix at the end of the section of tips for using Solver.

Unprotecting locked cells: If you want to make changes to locked cells or if you want to unprotect the spreadsheet for certain Solver runs, go to the **Tools** menu, select **Protection**, and click **Unprotect**.

Saving Excel files: If you want to save any of the Excel spreadsheets that you modify, save it in the same directory (default: C:\Program Files\MktgEng\Excel) in which the other Excel files are located.

Non US Versions of Excel: Much of our code assumes that you will be using English/American conventions for numbers and currency. The most critical problem is the difference between the use of the "." and the "," to refer to decimals depending on the country you are in. You must use US conventions in your input and you must make the following system modifications to run the programs with a non-US version of Excel.

First, Close any open programs.

Next, Click the **Start Button**, point to **Settings**, click **Control Panel**.

Next, Double Click Regional Settings.

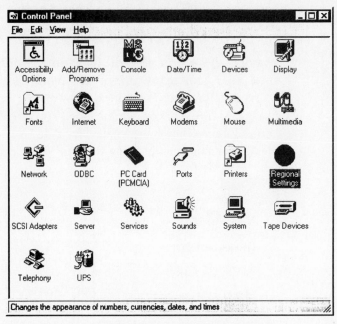

Select English (United States) as indicated below and first click **Apply** and then **OK**:

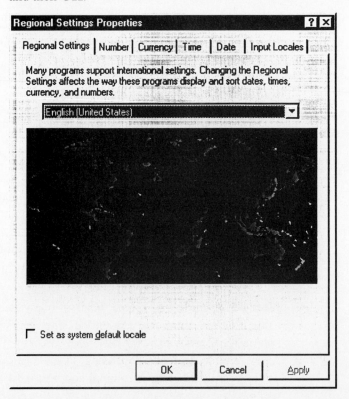

(You may be requested to insert the Windows CD at this time.)

Select the Number and Currency tabs and check to see that the US conventions are now applied.

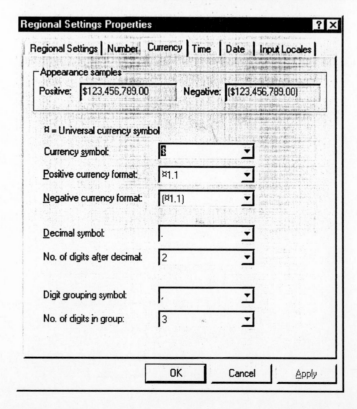

After you have completed these changes, Click the **Start Button** again, then click **Shut Down** and Click **Restart the Computer** and finally Click **OK**.

This procedure will allow you to run our software.

Be sure to reset to your local conventions when you are done using our software!

NOTE: *The following tips apply only to software modules that run directly off the main menu, namely, Cluster Analysis, Multinomial Logit Analysis, and Positioning Analysis.*

Incorporating your own data sets: There are three ways to create new data sets for Cluster Analysis, Multinomial Logit Analysis, and Positioning Analysis.

1. **Load an ASCII file containing the data in the appropriate format**: Use a standard word processing program to generate a text file that can be directly read by the program. The format for the file follows:

Perceptual Mapping	Line 1
3 4	Line 2
5.6 6.0 4.6 3.6 4.4 3.6 5.2 2.2 2.9 6.4 2.7 2.6	Section 1
Sprint MCI AT&T Other	Section 2
Value Service Special Programs	Section 3

   Line 1: Enter title of data set
   Line 2: Enter the number of rows and the number of columns of data
   Section 1: Enter the data (separate by comma or space)
   Section 2: Enter column headings
   Section 3: Enter row headings

   You can load this file into Marketing Engineering by selecting **File**, followed by **Open**. You will be prompted for the file name.

2. **Import data from Excel**: First, open the Marketing Engineering program. From the **File** menu, select **New**.

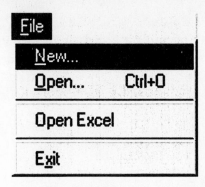

Enter a file name and click **OK** to see the following screen.

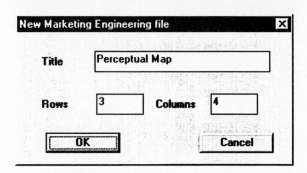

Enter a title for the data and the number of rows and columns. Click **OK.**

Next, separately enter or import a data set into Excel (just the data, no labels) as shown below:

	A	B	C	D	E
1	5.6	6	4.6	3.6	
2	4.4	3.6	5.2	2.2	
3	2.9	6.4	2.7	2.6	
4					

You can now import the data from Excel into Marketing Engineering in one of the following two ways:

Copy and paste the data directly into Marketing Engineering. In Excel, select the data range you want to import into Marketing Engineering. From the **Edit** menu use **Copy** or **Cut** to paste the data to Windows clipboard. Use the ALT+TAB key combination to get to the Marketing Engineering window. Place the cursor on the first row and first column of the blank spreadsheet and paste the data from Excel onto the Marketing Engineering worksheet. If you want to override the default column and row headings, enter the new names by selecting Marketing Engineering's **Edit** menu and then **Edit Row Labels** or **Edit Column Labels**.

Import as an Excel 4.0 file: Save the data as an Excel 4.0 worksheet. Go to the **File** menu in Marketing Engineering and select **Import Excel**. You will be prompted for the file name.

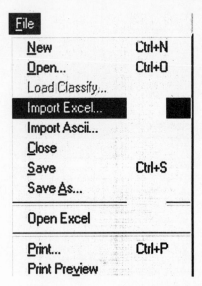

3. *Import just data from an ASCII file*: First open the Marketing Engineering program. From the **File** menu, select **New**. You will be prompted to provide a title for the data and the number of rows and columns.

    Now load a text file that contains just the data (the 3×4 data set above), one record per line with data separated by a space or tab. Position the cursor on the first row and first column of the spreadsheet. On the **File** menu, select **Import ASCII**. You will prompted for the file name.

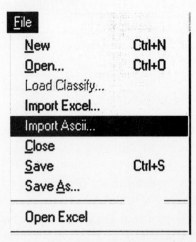

If you wish to override the default column and row headings, enter the new names directly on the spreadsheet by going to the **Edit** menu and selecting **Edit Row Labels** or **Edit Column Labels**.

4. ***Enter the data manually***: On the **File** menu click **New**. You will be prompted to provide a title for the data and the number of rows and columns. Next you can enter data in the blank spreadsheet starting with the first column of the first row.

Viewing the data: Once you have entered or imported data into Marketing Engineering, you will see a graphical display of the data.

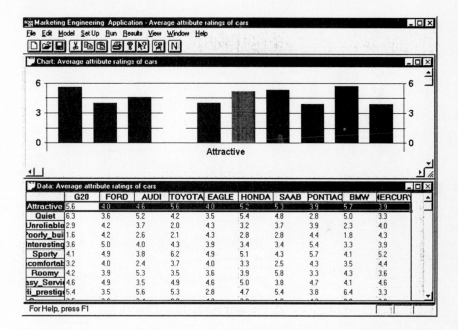

By clicking on a column or row header on the spreadsheet you can obtain a graphical display of the data in that column or row. You can also simultaneously display any subset of the data by dragging the mouse over the desired cells. On the **Edit** menu, you can use **Insert** and **Delete** to make changes to the data.

Changing row and column labels: On the **Edit** menu use **Edit Row Labels** and **Edit Column Labels** to make changes.

Modifying data: You can make changes to the data directly on the spreadsheet. These changes will be incorporated the next time you run the model. However the changes will not be saved for the future unless you specifically save them by going to the **File** menu and choosing **Save** or **Save As**.

Description of the Icons on Marketing Engineering toolbar. On the main window of Marketing Engineering, you will see the following toolbar:

Below is a short description of the each of the items on the toolbar:

Tool	Description

Creates a new marketing engineering data worksheet.

Opens an existing marketing engineering data worksheet.

Saves the currently loaded file.

Cuts a selection and places it on the Windows clipboard.

Copies a selection to the clipboard.

Pastes the contents of the clipboard.

Prints the active data worksheet according to the current print settings.

Displays marketing engineering version and copyright information.

Opens the main help file for marketing engineering.

Runs the selected program (Cluster Analysis, Multinomial Logit Analysis, or Positioning Analysis).

Displays next chart in Positioning Analysis and Multinomial Logit Analysis.

APPENDIX
Tips for Using Solver

The Solver implemented in Excel (produced by a software firm called Frontline Systems) uses numerical methods to solve equations and to optimize linear and nonlinear functions with either continuous variables (as in advertising spending) or integer variables (number of account-visits in a quarter). The methods used are iterative; generally Solver calculates how small changes in the decision variables affect the value of the objective function. If the objective function improves (e.g., if profit increases), Solver moves the decision variables in that direction. If the objective function gets worse, Solver moves in the opposite direction. If the objective function cannot be improved by either an increase or a decrease in any of the decision variables, Solver stops, reporting at least a local solution. In using Solver, you should be aware of the following situations that might occur:

1. **Local optima**: While Solver may have found the top of a hill (the highest point in the region), there may be a higher peak elsewhere. Solver would have to go DOWN from the local peak and begin searching elsewhere to find it. In other words, Solver would need a new starting value ("By Changing Variable" cells in the "Solver Parameter" box) to find the optimum.

   Example: The following is an S-shaped advertising spending function to be optimized. Suppose that we started Solver with the level of advertising = 0. Note that advertising spending cannot be negative and that profit initially decreases with increases in advertising spending because we have an advertising response model with a threshold. Hence Solver cannot decrease advertising spending to less than zero (because of the constraint) and it does not want to go up (as, locally, at least, that would decrease profitability), and so we are at a local maximum. However, if we start the problem with advertising at 1.0 or greater, Solver will correctly find the optimum value at $7.25.

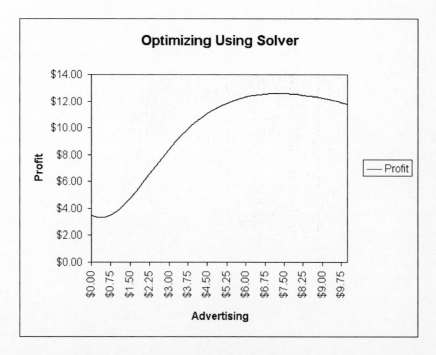

What this example illustrates is that when you are using Solver, you may need to try different starting values to be sure that you have reached a global optimal solution. Some of our Excel spreadsheets have built-in options that permit you to try a different starting value if Solver fails to converge or gives you a local solution.

2. **No feasible solution**: Suppose that we set two constraints: $X > 6$ and $X < 3$. Clearly both of these constraints cannot be satisfied at the same time, and Solver will fail to provide any solution. While the example here makes the lack of any fea sible solution obvious, in larger problems this is often quite subtle.

3. **Other problems**: General nonlinear optimizers like Excel's Solver are remarkable technical additions to the analyst's toolkit. With their power and flexibility come a variety of other problems, however. The user who wants to use Solver directly in market analyses or who wants to adapt or adjust the operation of some of the software that uses Solver may run into a number of other questions or problems, many of which are addressed in Excel's User's Guide.

   Some of those problems are caused by the way the user formulates the specific problem and employs Solver's options. Other problems may be caused by bugs in your version as of Excel and in Excel's link to your operating system (your version of Windows). If the results you are getting do not make sense, it may help to quit Windows or even to reboot your computer before trying to solve the problem again.

Chapter 1

TUTORIAL FOR CLUSTER ANALYSIS

Concept

Markets are heterogeneous. Customers differ in their values, needs, wants, constraints, beliefs, and incentives to act in a particular way. Products compete with one another in attempting to satisfy the needs and wants of those customers. By segmenting the market, firms can better understand their customers and target their marketing efforts efficiently and effectively. Through segmentation, an organization strives to attain a happy middle ground where it does not rely on a common marketing program for all customers, nor does it incur the high costs of developing a unique program for each customer.

Three definitions are critical to the concept of segmentation:

A *market segment* is a group of actual or potential customers who can be expected to respond in a similar way to a product or service offer. That is, they want the same types of benefits or solutions to problems from the product or service, or they respond in a similar way to a company's marketing communications.

Market segmentation is the process of dividing customers whose valuations of a product or service vary greatly into groups or segments containing customers whose valuations vary very little within the group but vary greatly among groups.

A *target market* is a market that a company chooses to serve effectively and profitably.

There is no single segmentation approach. The marketing problem, the timing, the availability of relevant data, and similar considerations should dictate the appropriate approach.

If the firm has data on customer characteristics (e.g., needs) from a sample of customers, then it can use Cluster Analysis to identify the appropriate segments. Cluster analysis is a set of techniques for discovering structure (groupings) within a complex body of data, such as the data used in segmentation analysis. We can explain the concept by considering a deck of cards. Each card varies from the other cards along three dimensions (variables): suit, color, and number. If you are asked to partition a pack of cards into two distinct groups, you might sort them into red and black, or into numbered cards and picture cards. While you can partition a pack of cards intuitively, partitioning a large number of items into groups can be very complex, especially if those items vary along a number of different dimensions. To form segments in such cases, we have to use formal methods. There are two basic classes of methods:

- Hierarchical methods, in which you build up or break down the data customer by customer (row by row)
- Partitioning methods, in which you break the data into a pre-specified number of segments and then reallocate or swap customers to improve some measure of effectiveness

Our software includes one method of each type—Ward's (1963) (hierarchical) and *K*-means (partitioning).

Hierarchical methods produce "trees" formally called dendograms. Hierarchical methods themselves fall into two categories: build-up (agglomerative) methods and split-down (divisive) methods.

Agglomerative methods generally follow this procedure:

1. At the beginning you consider each item (customer) to be its own cluster.

2. You join the two items that are closest on some chosen measure of distance.

3. You then join the next two closest objects (individual items or clusters), either joining two items to form a group or attaching an item to the existing cluster.

4. Return to step 3 until all items are clustered.

Agglomerative methods differ in how they join clusters to one another. In Ward's method, one of the two methods included in the software, you form clusters based on the change in the error sum of squares associated with joining any pair of clusters.

The most commonly used partitioning method is K-means clustering. The procedure works as follows:

1. Begin with two cluster centers (starting points) and allocate every item (customer) to its nearest cluster center.

2. Reallocate items one at a time to reduce the sum of internal cluster variability until you have minimized the criterion (the sum of the within-cluster-sums of squares) for two clusters.

3. Repeat steps 1 and 2 for three, four, or more clusters.

4. After completing step 3, return to step 1 and repeat the procedure with different starting points until the process converges – you no longer see decreases in the within-cluster sum of squares.

While there are many ways to determine starting points, we recommend using the output of Ward's procedure to give good starting points (this is the procedure used in our software).

In addition to Cluster Analysis, our software includes two associated procedures: (1) Factor Analysis and (2) Discriminant Analysis. In Factor Analysis we reduce a large data set into a smaller data set. Specifically, we analyze the interrelationships among a large number of variables and then represent them in terms of common, underlying factors. Such data reduction is sometimes required in segmentation studies because we have data on a wide battery of attitude and needs variables from a sample of customers. If many of those variables measure similar or interrelated constructs, then the subsequent segmentation analysis could lead to misleading conclusions because some variables are overweighted and others underweighted. In Discriminant Analysis, we identify observable characteristics of customers (e.g., sex, area of residence, media habits, etc.) that maximally discriminate between customers in different segments. By identifying such variables, we will be better able to develop marketing programs to targeted segments.

Software

To run Cluster Analysis, you must have a data file structured so that the rows are customers and the columns are the variables that reflect the preferences or needs of those customers (the segmentation basis variables. If you select the discriminant analysis option, you must identify a second separate data file with the same number of rows (referring to the customers) but possibly with a different number of columns (which reflect the segment descriptors). The needs data and the descriptor data are kept in two separate files to ensure that segmentation criteria and targeting criteria need not, and often will not, be the same.

We illustrate the use of the program below, referring to the exercise on Conglomerate's new PDA. The exercise concerns identifying need-based segments for a new type of Personal Digital Assistant (PDA) and finding a way to target the selected segments. The data for this exercise are in two files:

- PDA.DAT contains information on the needs of sampled customers.
- PDA_DIS.DAT contains information on demographics and other variables relevant to developing a program for targeting a PDA to these customers.

From the **Model** menu, select **Cluster Analysis**. You will be prompted to choose the file containing input data. Use the file PDA.DAT for the exercise. This will load the data into the program.

NOTE: *If you make changes to the data to evaluate alternative solutions, the program will not automatically save these changes. Save the changes (under a separate file name if necessary) by going to the* **File** *menu and clicking* **Save As**.

Go to the **Set Up** menu to select the parameters for your analysis as shown in the following example:

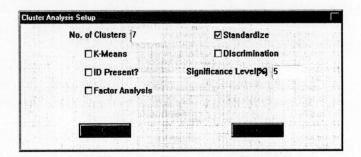

In the area for **No. of Clusters,** you can choose between two and nine clusters (segments) for analysis. If you choose **Standardize**, all variables will be standardized to 0 mean and unit variance before analysis. Choosing this option is a good idea if the variables are measured on different scales, as is the price variable in this example. **Discrimination** allows you to maximally discriminate among the resulting segments using the demographic variables available in PDA_DIS.DAT (the program will prompt you to indicate this file name when needed). **ID Present** allows you to label a case in the data. Such identification is useful in developing segment-specific marketing programs.

NOTE: *The* **ID Present** *option is disabled in this educational version of the software.*

As a default, this program uses the Ward's minimum-variance hierarchical-clustering analysis. By selecting **K-Means,** you can run a K-Means clustering algorithm. In this case, the output of hierarchical clustering provides the initial configuration for the K-Means clustering. After you select the options for the run, click **OK**.

If you check **Factor Analysis,** the program will preprocess your input data to identify a set of factors, which it then uses in the cluster analysis procedure. Factor analysis will standardize the variables before finding the underlying factors. However the resulting factor scores, which are then used for cluster analysis, are not standardized. We recommend that you use unstandardized factor scores in the cluster analysis procedure. Thus, you should not check **Standardize** in the setup box.

Next go to the **Run** menu and select **Run Model**. If you selected **Factor Analysis,** you will see the following dialog box that asks you to select the number of factors you want to retain for the cluster analysis procedure (this allows you to override the number of factors recommended by the program).

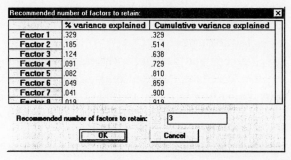

After the program runs, you will see the results of the analysis displayed in the top window. To see the output more clearly, you can maximize this window. In this example, the resulting screen displays the members of the five segments.

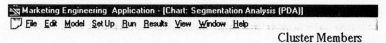

Cluster Members

1   1 4 11 13 28 37 38 42 44 54 62 70 71

2   2 3 5 12 15 18 21 25 27 31 45 48 50 58 59 60 66 67 69 72

3   6 8 16 24 36 39 43 47 49 52 53 55 56 57 61 63 65

4   7 14 20 26 34 35 51 64

5   9 10 17 19 22 23 29 30 32 33 40 41 46 68

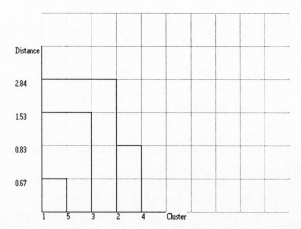

If you scroll down the window, you will see a dendogram showing the distances between the clusters. If you want to remove the grids from the dendogram, go to the **View** menu, choose **View Options**, and clear the check box for **Grid**. (The dendogram is displayed only if you did not choose the K-Means clustering option.)

In this example, clusters 1 and 5 are the closest clusters, separated by a distance of 0.67 units; clusters 2 and 4 are separated by 0.83 units; and clusters 1 and 3 are separated by 1.53 units. If you decide on a four-cluster solution, the two nearest clusters (1 and 5) will be merged into one cluster. Use the dendogram to select an appropriate number of clusters. (One way to determine the number of clusters is to look for a solution in which the clusters are separated evenly). You can combine clusters that are close to each other by specifying a solution that contains fewer clusters.

You can add descriptive labels to the dendogram. Click anywhere on the screen, and a label dialog box will appear. What you enter in this dialog box will be inserted at the selected location. To delete the labels you entered, go to the **Edit** menu and choose **Delete Labels**.

Marketing Engineering Application - [Chart: Segmentation Analysis (PDA)]

File Edit Model Set Up Run Results View Window Help

Correlation of variables with each significant discriminant function
(significance level < .05).

Variable	Func1	Func2	Func3
PDA	.696	.154	.136
Professnl	.682	.063	.264
Income	.660	.099	.203
Bus_Week	.600	-.040	-.023
Education	.553	.021	-.142
M_Gourmet	.464	.069	.184
PC_Mag	.294	.002	.114
Construct	-.300	.670	-.177
Field&Stre	-.245	.552	.110
Emergency	-.184	.481	.038
Age	-.043	-.061	.057
Service	-.334	-.401	.718
Sales	-.106	-.439	-.638
%_Variance Explained	41.4	35.1	17.5

For Help, press F1

EXHIBIT 1

Exhibit 1 shows the correlation between each variable and the statistically significant discriminant functions. (This is displayed only if you selected **Discrimination** in the **Set Up** box.) The *absolute magnitude* of this correlation indicates the extent to which a variable discriminates between the clusters. The correlations are ordered from the largest to the smallest in absolute magnitude within each discriminant function. In this example, whether someone is a professional is an important descriptor of the cluster to which that person belongs. The "Professional" variable correlates highly with a discriminant function (Function 1) that explains 41.4 percent of the variation among the respondents included in the study.

To print a copy of the summary results to an attached printer, go to **File** and choose **Print**. To cut and paste these results as an object in another Windows application (e.g., Word for Windows), bring the display window to the foreground, go to the **Edit** menu and select **Cut** or **Copy** and then paste into another Windows application.

You can view an extensive set of associated diagnostics (means of variables in each segment, hit rate, etc.) by going to the **Results** menu and selecting **View Diagnostics**.

If you selected **Factor Analysis,** the first set of diagnostics that you would see is the following table showing variance explained by each factor, the factor score matrix, and the factor-loading matrix.

Diagnostics for factor analysis

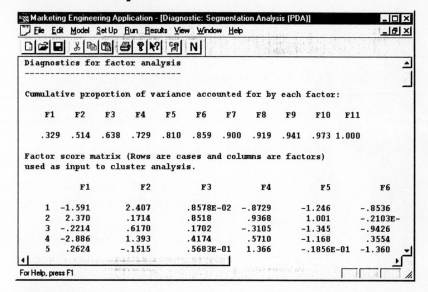

EXHIBIT 2

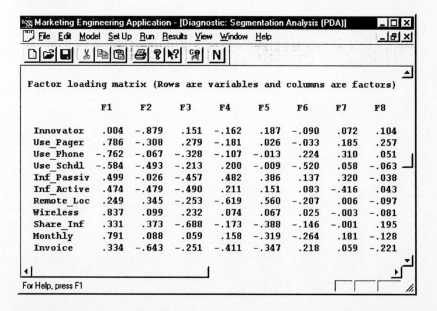

EXHIBIT 3

Diagnostics for cluster analysis

If you did not select **K-Means** in the **Set Up** box, you will see the table shown below for the hierarchical-clustering procedure (Ward's method).

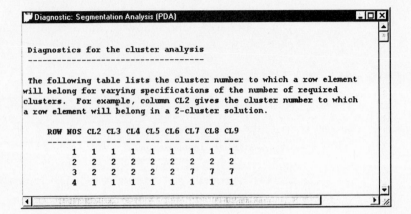

EXHIBIT 4

Exhibit 4 lists the cluster to which a row element (customer) will belong for varying specifications of the number of clusters. For example, row 3 will belong to cluster 2 as long as you specify fewer than seven clusters. If you specify more than seven clusters, this customer will be assigned to cluster 7.

If you selected **K-Means** in the **Set Up** box, you will see the table shown in exhibit 5, giving the probabilities of each row element belonging to each cluster. The probabilities are in inverse proportion to the distance between a customer's characteristics and cluster centroids.

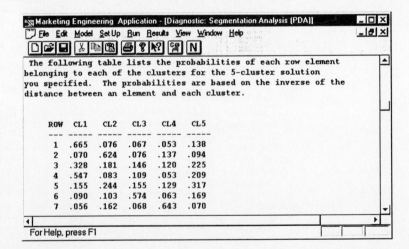

EXHIBIT 5

```
▓▒Marketing Engineering  Application - [Diagnostic: Segmentation Analysis (PDA)]    _□☒
  File  Edit  Model  Set Up  Run  Results  View  Window  Help                      _⊟☒
  ▭☞▤  ✂▤▥  ▤ ▓▨▣ ▨ [N]
 Actual                          Predicted cluster                              ▲
 Cluster     # of cases    CL1     CL2     CL3     CL4     CL5

   CL1          13           6       1       1       2       3
                           46.2%    7.7%    7.7%   15.4%   23.1%

   CL2          20           2      11       0       2       5
                           10.0%   55.0%    .0%    10.0%   25.0%

   CL3          17           2       0      13       1       1
                           11.8%    .0%    76.5%    5.9%    5.9%

   CL4          8            0       0       0       8       0
                            .0%     .0%     .0%   100.0%    .0%

   CL5          14           4       3       0       1       6
                           28.6%   21.4%    .0%     7.1%   42.9%

 Hit rate: Percent of total cases correctly classified: 61.11         ▼
 ◄                                                              ►
  For Help, press F1
```

EXHIBIT 6

Exhibit 6 presents a summary of the predictive validity of the discriminant analysis. The overall hit rate is the proportion of all individuals who are correctly assigned by the discriminant functions. The matrix indicates the predictive ability of the discriminant functions with respect to each cluster.

You can also see the mean of each needs variable in each cluster and the mean of each descriptor variable (if you had selected **Discrimination** in the **Set Up** box).

```
▓▒Marketing Engineering  Application - [Diagnostic: Segmentation Analysis (PDA)]    _□☒
  File  Edit  Model  Set Up  Run  Results  View  Window  Help                      _⊟☒
  ▭☞▤  ✂▤▥  ▤ ▓▨▣ ▨ [N]
 Means for each variable in each cluster:                                        ▲

   Variable    Overall      CL1        CL2        CL3        CL4        CL5
   ----------  ---------- ---------- ---------- ---------- ---------- ----------
 Innovator      3.63        1.77       3.60       5.82       3.25       2.93
 Use_Pager      3.46        2.15       4.70       3.65       4.88       1.86
 Use_Phone      3.72        4.69       2.30       4.53       2.25       4.71
 Use_Schdl      3.89        3.77       3.00       5.35       2.25       4.43
 Inf_Passiv     3.56        1.62       3.85       2.65       5.63       4.86
 Inf_Active     4.01        2.38       3.95       4.53       5.13       4.36
 Remote_Loc     4.50        4.54       4.80       3.88       5.00       4.50
 Wireless       2.90        1.46       5.10       1.65       5.25       1.29
 Share_Inf      3.40        3.38       3.10       2.47       5.75       3.64
 Monthly       20.3        12.7       31.0       10.9       40.6       11.8
 Invoice       993.        527.       755.      .159E+04   .191E+04   521.   ▼
 ◄                                                              ►
  For Help, press F1
```

EXHIBIT 7

Once you settle on a solution you may wish to name the clusters for identification and for generating reports. Choose names that seem to best characterize those clusters. On the **Edit** menu click **Edit Cluster Labels** and enter the appropriate names in the boxes provided.

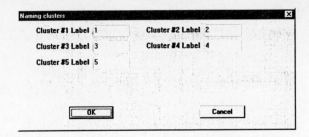

Once you complete cluster analysis, you can use the results of the completed analysis to classify any number of new cases according to the discriminant functions. This ability to assign a large database of customers to selected target segments based on a smaller study sample enhances the implementability of the segmentation study. First, load a file containing demographic information about the new cases. For the purposes of this tutorial you may use PDA_DIS.DAT for classification. Go to the **File** menu and click **Load Classify**.

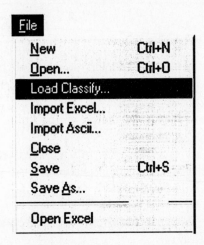

Next, go to the **Run** menu and click **Classify**.

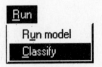

This will display the results of the classification analysis on the spreadsheet, showing the segment to which each new case was assigned. Here case 1 is assigned to cluster 1, case 3 to cluster 2, etc.

Marketing Engineering Application - [Data: Targeting analysis (PDA)]

File Edit Model Set Up Run Results View Window Help

	Age	Education	Income	Construct	mergenc	Sales	Service	Professnl
1 => 1	32.0	3.0	20.0	0.0	0.0	0.0	0.0	0.0
2 => 2	42.0	3.0	47.0	0.0	0.0	0.0	1.0	0.0
3 => 2	22.0	3.0	28.0	0.0	0.0	0.0	1.0	0.0
4 => 1	46.0	2.0	45.0	0.0	0.0	1.0	0.0	0.0
5 => 2	54.0	2.0	51.0	0.0	0.0	0.0	1.0	0.0
6 => 3	25.0	4.0	81.0	0.0	0.0	0.0	0.0	1.0
7 => 4	46.0	1.0	25.0	1.0	0.0	0.0	0.0	0.0
8 => 3	33.0	3.0	42.0	0.0	0.0	0.0	0.0	1.0
9 => 5	35.0	4.0	30.0	0.0	0.0	0.0	0.0	1.0
10 => 1	51.0	1.0	41.0	0.0	0.0	1.0	0.0	0.0

For Help, press F1

Limitations of the educational version of the software

Maximum number of variables: 15
Maximum number of observations: 200
Maximum number of clusters: 9
Nominal variables: Cannot use nominal data in cluster analysis, but you could use nominal variables (dummy coded) in discriminant analysis.

References

Dillon, William R. and Goldstein, Matthew 1984, *Multivariate Analysis: Methods and Applications*, John Wiley & Sons, New York.

Hartigan, J. A. and Wong, M. A. 1979, "K-Means Algorithm," *Applied Statistics*, Vol. 28, No. 1, pp. 100-108.

Lilien, Gary L. and Rangaswamy, Arvind 1998, *Marketing Engineering: Computer-Assisted Marketing Analysis and Planning*, Chapter 3, Addison Wesley Longman, Reading, Massachusetts.

Moriarty, Rowland T. and Reibstein, David J. 1982, *Benefit Segmentation: An Industrial Application*, Report No. 82-110, Marketing Science Institute, Cambridge, Massachusetts.

Murtagh, F. 1985, *Multidimensional Clustering Algorithms* (CompStat Lectures 4), Physica-Verlag, Würzburg/Wien.

Ward, J. 1963 "Hierarchical Grouping to Optimize an Objective Function," *Journal of the American Statistical Association,* Vol. 58, pp. 236-244.

CONGLOMERATE INC'S NEW PDA CASE

Conglomerate Inc.'s new PDA (1995)

The cellular phone division of Conglomerate Inc. has teamed up with a PC manufacturer to develop, produce, and market a novel hybrid combination of a personal digital assistant (PDA) and a "smart" cellular phone. They have tentatively named it **ConneCtor**. It transmits and receives both data and voice (unlike competing PDAs which focus on data).

ConneCtor
Another Conglomerate Success Story?

ConneCtor is lightweight and is shaped like a portable phone with a small backlit LCD touch screen along the handset. Its (open) operating system performs standard cellphone functions and such personal information management (PIM) functions as a calendar, calculator, and address book. It can send and receive faxes, voice messages, and e-mail. Users can input data in four ways:

- By typing on the screen keyboard
- By using a numerical keyboard
- By writing on the screen in "digital ink"
- By speaking into the phone (it includes voice recognition software)

The voice recognition feature is based on a neural network that is trained to recognize a particular user's voice patterns. An additional feature unique to **ConneCtor** is linkage via wireless local area networks to other PDA's.

In summary, the features of Conglomerate's handheld device are

- Instant communication from PDA to PDA
- Cellular phone and pager, fax and e-mail
- Calendar, scheduler, calculator, and address book
- An open system for customized applications
- A paperless note pad
- Voice recognition

Conglomerate is now trying to identify segments within the market for PDAs, target appropriate segment(s) for **ConneCtor,** and position **ConneCtor** in the chosen segments.

Background on the PDA market

In August 1993, Apple introduced its Newton PDA. The broad acceptance that Apple had anticipated did not materialize, and Apple sold only 80,000 Newtons that year. In 1995, the PDA appeared to be on the verge of greater growth and development. The PDA market had grown in four areas: specialized vertical applications (e.g., physician scheduling), PIM (Personal Information Management), mobile communications, and as a supplementary gateway into the Internet.

Even though it has four main applications, the PDA is primarily targeted at "road warriors" or "mobile professionals." This group consists of approximately 25 million people in the United States, of whom about 5 million travel with a computer notebook. Many of these individuals already have cellular phones and must send and receive a large number of messages and data. The standard PDA cannot handle their needs.

The survey

Conglomerate, Inc. hired a market research firm to survey the market across a broad range of occupation types. The survey includes a screening item asking respondents if they had or would consider a

PDA. Only those respondents who answered affirmatively to that question were retained for further analysis.

The questionnaire

The questionnaire asked the respondents to provide data on two kinds of variables: segmentation basis or needs variables and variables that could be used in describing or targeting the clusters using discriminant analysis.

Questions for determining segmentation-basis variables

X1   Whenever new technologies emerge in my field, I am among the first to adopt them.
       (1 = Strongly disagree......7 = Strongly agree)
    How often do you use the following:
       (1 = Never......7 = Always)

X2   a. Pager?

X3   b. Phone or voice mail?

X4   c. Scheduling or contact-management tools, i.e., filofax or similar devices?

X5   How often do others send you time-sensitive information (e.g., work orders)?
       (1 = Never......7 = Daily)

X6   How often do you have to send time-sensitive information while away from your office?
       (1 = Never ...... 7 = Daily)

X7   How much of your time do you spend away from your office location?
       (1 = 0 %......7 = 70% or more)

X8   How important is wireless communication to you?
       (1 = Not at all important.....7 = Very important)

X9   How important is it for you to share information rapidly with colleagues while away from an office location?
       (1 = Not at all important......7 = Very important)
    How much would you be willing to pay for a personal digital assistant (PDA) with the following features: instant communication from PDA to PDA, cellular phone and pager, fax and e-mail, calendar, scheduler, calculator, address book, open system for customized applications, paperless note pad, and voice recognition?

X10   a. Monthly (for all services that you use)?

X11   b. Invoice price for the PDA device with all features?

Questions for determining variables for discriminant analysis

Z1	Age
Z2	Education (1 = High school, 2 = Some college, 3 = College, 4 = Graduate degree)
Z3	Income

Type of industry or occupation:
(0 = No, 1 = Yes)

Z4	Construction
Z5	Emergency (fire, police, ambulance, etc.)
Z6	Sales (insurance, pharmacy, etc.)
Z7	Maintenance and service
Z8	Professional (e.g., lawyer, consultant, etc.)
Z9	Do you own a PDA?

Media consumption (Readership of magazines):
(0 = No, 1 = Yes)

Z10	*Businessweek*
Z11	*PC Magazine*
Z12	*Field & Stream*
Z13	*Modern Gourmet*

EXERCISES

1. Run only cluster analysis (without **Discrimination**) on the data to try to identify the number of distinct segments present in this market. Consider both the distances separating the segments and the characteristics of the resulting segments.

2. Identify and profile (name) the clusters that you select. Given the attributes of **ConneCtor**, which cluster would you target for your marketing campaign?

3. Go back to **Set Up**, check **Discrimination**, and rerun the analysis. How would you go about targeting the segment(s) you picked in question 2?

4. How has this analysis helped you to segment the market for **ConneCtor?**

5. What other analyses would you do to develop a marketing program for **ConneCtor**? Indicate both the type of data you would collect (if any) and the types of analyses you would conduct.

Chapter 2

TUTORIAL FOR MULTINOMIAL LOGIT ANALYSIS

Concept

In recent years, many companies have built extensive databases containing individual-level data. For example, companies such as American Express and AT&T have detailed information on demographics and purchase patterns of their customers. Likewise, many supermarkets have data from scanner panels, where a panel of consumers uses specially issued cards for their shopping. This technology allows supermarkets to store and track all purchases—captured by bar-code scanners—made by a panel member. Analyses of these data can help managers to infer how various variables (e.g., price) influence the choices that customers make. Based on these analyses, firms can develop marketing programs that are tailored to specific market segments, or even tailored to individual customers.

One of the most powerful models to have emerged in recent years to analyze individual-level choice data is the multinomial logit (MNL) model. For example, customers may have a choice of five detergents. In the MNL model, typically the dependent variable is choice—the brand of detergent a customer bought when faced with a choice of these detergents. The independent variables influencing this choice could be price, promotion (whether a detergent was on promotion), product characteristics such as whether a detergent is scent-free, etc. If we have such data from a number of customers over a single purchase occasion or over multiple purchase occasions, we can specify an MNL model as follows:

$$P_{i1} = \frac{e^{A_{i1}}}{\Sigma_j e^{A_{ij}}} \qquad (1)$$

where:

A_{ij} = Attractiveness of alternative j to customer i, $= \Sigma_k w_k b_{ijk}$

b_{ijk} = the value (observed or measured) of variable k for alternative j when customer i made a purchase;

w_k = derived importance weight associated with variable k;

P_{i1} = The probability that customer i will choose alternative 1. Analogous equations can be specified for the probabilities of customer i choosing the other alternatives.

We use the model to determine w_k and P_{ij} using a statistical estimation technique called maximum likelihood. That is, we determine w_k such that the sample pattern of choices that we observe is the most likely sample to have occurred, under a given probability model. Once w_k are estimated, P_{ij} can be computed for each alternative for each customer by applying equation (1).

The MNL model has several attractive features:

1. The model is consistent with rational choice behavior. Customers are assumed to select that alternative that gives them the highest utility, i.e., the one that is most attractive. However, the attractiveness of the alternatives to each customer is not known to the modeler, and is therefore treated as a random variable. This means that the choice probability of alternative j is equal to the probability that the attractiveness of alternative j, A_{ij}, is greater than or equal to the attractiveness of all other alternatives in the choice set.

2. The model satisfies the sum and range constraints, i.e., the probability of choosing any alternative lies between 0 and 1 (range constraint) and the sum of probabilities over all choice alternatives is equal to 1 (sum constraint). Purchase probabilities at the individual customer level is equivalent to market share at the market level; indeed by summing purchase probabilities across customers (suitably weighted for differences in purchase quantities, purchase timing, and the like), one gets an estimate of market share. So, the derived market shares also satisfy the sum and range constraints.

3. The structure of the MNL model mirrors the differential sensitivities we expect in actual choice behavior. To see why this is so, consider the properties of the model. Graphing equation (1) as a function of A_{ij} produces an S-Shaped curve, tracking the expected relationship between attractiveness and choice – the curve asymptotes to zero for unattractive alternatives and to 1 for very attractive ones. Further the marginal sensitivities (the rate of change of choice probabilities with a change in the value of an independent variable) is highest for a choice probability of 50%, but approaches 0 when the choice probability is close to zero or one. Thus, the model has the nice behavioral property that the incremental impact of an independent variable is at its peak when the customer is "on the fence" about choosing it.

The major disadvantages of the MNL model are the property of "proportional draw" and the assumption that all customers consider all the alternatives included in the model. The proportional draw property implies that if a new choice alternative is introduced into the model, it will draw shares from all the existing alternatives in proportion to their current choice probabilities. This means that if you prefer light beers to regular beers, then adding a new regular beer to your choice set would nevertheless lower your probability of choosing a light beer, a counter-intuitive result. There are more sophisticated versions of the MNL model (e.g., the nested MNL model) that helps overcome these limitations.

Software

This software implements the non-nested multinomial logit model. The input data should have a particular structure for this program. The first column is the choice variable having a 1 or 0 (purchase or no purchase) for each alternative under consideration. The remaining columns of data correspond to independent variables, one for each column, including dummy variables, if any. The rows correspond to "cases." Each case (e.g., customer) consists of two or more contiguous rows, one for each alternative, where the first column indicates whether that customer chose that alternative (dependent variable) and the remaining columns indicate the data values for each of the independent variables included in the model. Optionally, each case can consist of multiple observations (e.g., purchases made over several purchase occasions). When there is more than one observation per case, the observation sets must be organized sequentially. If there are N alternatives, M cases, and P observations per case, then the total number of rows of data would be N*M*P.

NOTE: *For each case, only one alternative is chosen, i.e., has a choice value equal to 1.*

The following shows how the data are organized for analysis:

1. If you have more than 2 choice alternatives, organize the input data as shown below. The Choice variable column indicates whether a particular choice alternative was chosen by a customer (case) on a particular choice occasion and the remaining columns contain values of the independent variables for each choice alternative for each case. The screen below illustrates this data organization from the sample data file ABBLOGIT.DAT.

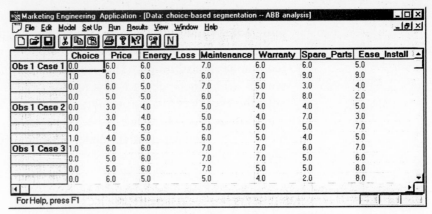

2. If you have two choice alternatives, the data is organized as shown below for the special case of the "binary logit" model. Each customer (case) consists of two alternatives, one of which has a Choice variable value equal to 0 and the other has a value equal to 1. The remaining columns in the data represent independent variables that explain the choices made by customers. In binary logit analysis, one of the choice alternatives serves as a reference—here, for convenience, the reference values of the independent variables are set to zero for the second choice alternative for each customer. The screen below illustrates this data organization from the file BBBC.DAT.

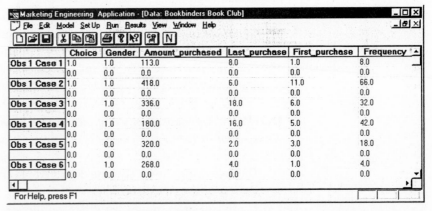

To enter the names of the available alternatives, go to the **Edit** menu and choose **Edit Row Labels**. If you have *n* choice alternatives, enter the names of these alternatives in the first *n* rows.

NOTE: *If you make changes to the data to evaluate alternative solutions, the program will not automatically save these changes. You can save the changes (under a separate filename) by going to* **File** *menu and choosing* **Save As**.

The following example illustrates the use of binary logit analysis in Bookbinders Book Club exercise. From the **Model** menu, select **Multinomial Logit Analysis**. You will be prompted for a data file. For this example, use the file called BBBC.DAT. You will then see the following screen (fill in the numbers indicated):

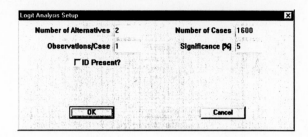

Number of Alternatives: Enter up to nine (choice) alternatives for analysis.

Number of Cases: Enter the number of cases for analysis.

Observations/Case: Indicate the number of observations per case. For example, if you observed choices of each customer over five purchase occasions, this option should be set to 5. The default value is 1.

Significance (%): Specify the significance level for the statistical tests. The program uses this to identify statistically significant coefficients from the analysis.

ID Present: This indicates whether a unique name is assigned to each customer. This option is disabled in the educational version.

    Click **OK**. To run the program, go to the **Run** menu and choose **Run Model**. After the program runs successfully, you will see a summary of the results in a sequence of screens, similar to the example below. Click **Back** and **Next** buttons to move back and forth among the screens. Click **Print** to get a print out of a screen.

NOTE: *The software implements the Newton method for determining the maximum likelihood estimates (Maddala, p.74). It is possible that this method may fail to yield estimates for some ill-conditioned data sets, where some sets of independent variables are highly correlated. In such cases, we recommend that you drop some of the correlated variables before conducting your analyses.*

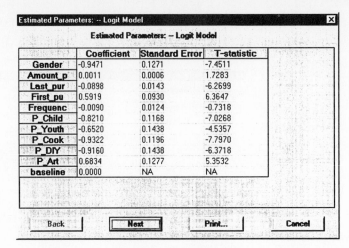

	Coefficient	Standard Error	T-statistic
Gender	-0.9471	0.1271	-7.4511
Amount_p	0.0011	0.0006	1.7283
Last_pur	-0.0898	0.0143	-6.2699
First_pu	0.5919	0.0930	6.3647
Frequenc	-0.0090	0.0124	-0.7318
P_Child	-0.8210	0.1168	-7.0268
P_Youth	-0.6520	0.1438	-4.5357
P_Cook	-0.9322	0.1196	-7.7970
P_DIY	-0.9160	0.1438	-6.3718
P_Art	0.6834	0.1277	5.3532
baseline	0.0000	NA	NA

After you look at the summary tables, you will see a graphical summary of the coefficients, elasticities, and predicted shares for each alternative:

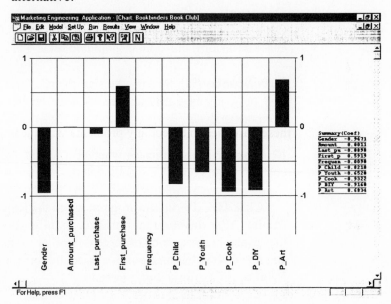

You can see one other chart that gives the market share forecasts for each alternative by going to the **Results** menu, choosing **Summary**, and then **View Next Chart** as shown below (Alternatively, click on the 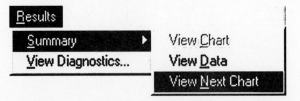 button on the Menu Bar).

You can also get additional statistical information about the results by going to the **Results** menu and selecting **View Diagnostics** menu option from the **Results** menu. The extensive set of diagnostics is organized into eight components.

Diagnostics—1

The first set of diagnostics you will see simply indicates the sizes of the data sets. The warning indicates that forecasting is based on the estimation sample, not on a separate holdout prediction sample. This is the only option available in the educational version of the software. The next piece of information indicates the number of rows of data (records) that the model processed.

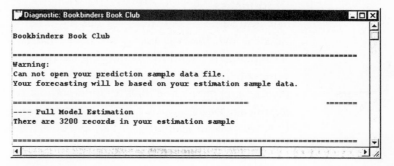

Diagnostics—2

Next, you will see a summary of the mean values of each variable for each alternative. If you use dummy variables, you can use the means of these variables to detect any problems with the data setup. In this example, the first choice alternative (Response) indicates whether someone responded to a direct mail campaign, and the second alternative is a dummy which we can ignore (all means are zero).

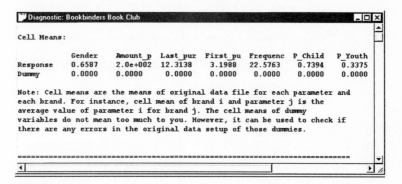

Diagnostics—3

The parameters of the logit model are estimated by a statistical procedure called maximum likelihood. The likelihood of a sample is measured by a likelihood function (or, more conventionally, a log-likelihood function). The iterative maximum likelihood procedure stops if one of the following three criteria is met (within a desired tolerance) for successive iterations: (1) the likelihood function does not improve, (2) the parameter estimates do not change, or (3) the search gradients do not change.

The history of the estimation summarizes what happened at each iteration:

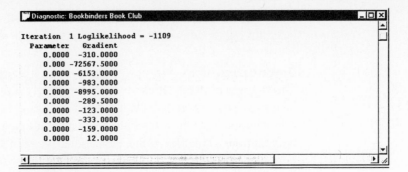

Diagnostics—4

The next set of diagnostics provides information about the parameter estimates and the variance-covariance matrix of the estimates. This information is useful for identifying the parameters that are significantly different from 0 in a statistical sense. You can interpret these coefficients in a manner similar to interpreting regression coefficients. A significant variable influences the choice probabilities of each alternative, whereas an insignificant variable does not offer much in the way of explaining the choices customers made.

NOTE: *These are asymptotic results—they are likely to be valid only if the sample is large.*

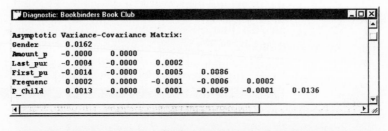

Diagnostics—5

The next set of diagnostics indicates the probability of each "case" (e.g., customer) selecting each of the alternatives and the hit rate, which is the percentage of cases for which the predicted choice (each case is assigned the alternative for which it has the highest probability) is equal to the known actual choice.

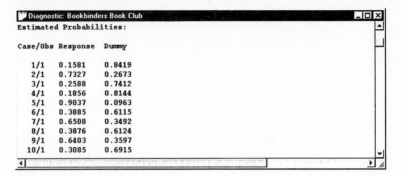

Diagnostics—6

The higher the hit rate, the higher the predictive ability of the model. If the estimation and prediction samples are not distinct (which is the case in the educational version of the software), then the hit rate is a measure of the goodness-of-fit rather than the predictive ability of the model.

In addition, the computed probabilities can be used to derive an estimate of the choice share of each alternative. (If a separate prediction sample is used, the choice shares are computed on that sample, rather than on the estimation sample. This option is not currently available in the educational version of the software.)

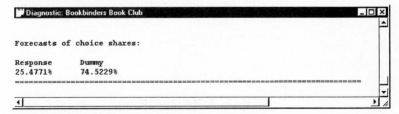

Diagnostics—7

The next set provides information about the elasticity of impact of each variable on choice shares. These are "arc" elasticities (i.e., not "point" elasticities). For each independent variable, the elasticity matrix refers to the following: the element in the (i,j)th position indicates the percentage change in the choice of alternative j for a one percent change of the variable for the *ith* alternative. For example, elements (1,1) and (1,2) in the following elasticity matrix for amount purchased are 0.1241 and −0.0424. This means that if we increase the amount purchased by a customer by one percent, then the share of the customers responding to the promotion would go up by 0.1241 percent and the share of customers not responding would go down by 0.0424 percent (Here, the magnitudes of these elasticities reflect the fact that only a fourth of the customers in the database responded to the direct mail offer.)

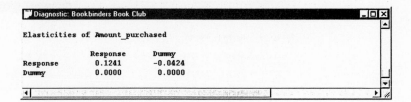

Diagnostics—8

Finally, we provide some statistics that can help you to evaluate how well the proposed model, the "full-parametric model," compares to 1) a "naive" model that assigns equal probabilities to all alternatives (i.e., all parameters are equal to 0) and 2) the constant model (i.e., all parameters except the constant term are zero). The reported Chi-square value is asymptotically distributed as a Chi-square distribution with the indicated degree of freedom (DF).

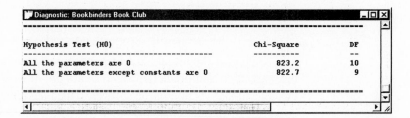

We also compute a Goodness-Of-Fit index that provides additional information about the performance of the model:

Rho-Square is similar to the R^2 measure in regression. It is an index of the extent to which the full parametric model performs better than the constant model. Rho-Bar-Square is another goodness-of-fit measure which is similar to "Adjusted R^2" in regression, which corrects for the number of parameters included in the full-parametric model.

Limitations of the educational version of the software

Number of observations:	3000
Number of variables:	20
Number of choice alternatives:	8
Number of observations per case:	10

References

Lilien, Gary L. and Rangaswamy, Arvind (1998), *Marketing Engineering: Computer-Assisted Marketing Analysis and Planning*, Chapter 2, Addison Wesley Longman, Reading, Massachusetts, pp. 42-47.

Maddala, G. S. (1983), *Limited Dependent and Qualitative Variables in Econometrics*, Cambridge University Press.

BOOKBINDERS BOOK CLUB CASE[1]

About 50,000 new titles, including new editions, are published in the U.S. each year, giving rise to a $20 billion book publishing industry (in 1994). About 10 percent of the books are sold through mail order.

Book retailing in the 1970s was characterized by the growth of chain bookstore operations in concert with the development of shopping malls. Traffic in bookstores in the 1980s was enhanced by the spread of discounting. In the 1990s, the superstore concept of book retailing has been responsible for the double-digit growth of the book industry. Generally situated near large shopping centers, superstores maintain large inventories of anywhere from 30,000 to 80,000 titles. Superstores are putting intense competitive pressure on book clubs, mail-order firms and retail outlets. Recently, on-line superstores, such as www.amazon.com, have emerged, carrying over 1 to 2.5 million titles and further intensifying the pressure on book clubs and mail-order firms. In response to these pressures, book clubs are starting to look at alternative business models that will make them more responsive to their customers' preferences.

Historically, book clubs offered their readers continuity and negative option programs that were based on an extended contractual relationship between the club and its subscribers. In a continuity program, popular in such genres as children's books, a reader signs up for an offer of several books for a few dollars each (plus shipping and handling on each book) and agrees to receive a shipment of one or two books each month thereafter. In a negative option program, subscribers get to choose which and how many additional books they will receive, but the default option is that the club's selection will be delivered to them each month. The club informs them of the monthly selection and they must mark "no" on their order forms if they do not want to receive it. Some firms are now beginning to offer books on a positive-option basis, but only to selected segments of their customer lists that they deem receptive to specific offers.

Book clubs are also beginning to use database-marketing techniques to work smarter rather than expand the coverage of their mailings. According to Doubleday president Marcus Willhelm, "the database is the key to what we are doing. We have to understand what our customers want and be more flexible. I doubt book clubs can survive if they offer the same 16 offers, the same fulfillment to everybody."[2] Doubleday uses modeling techniques to look at more than 80 variables, including geography and the types of books customers purchase, and selects three to five variables that are the most influential predictors.

---

[1] The case and the database were developed by Professors Nissan Levin and Jacob Zahavi at Tel Aviv University. We have adapted these materials for use with our software, with their permission.

[2] DM News, May 23, 1994.

The Bookbinders Book Club

The BBB Club was established in 1986 for the purpose of selling specialty books through direct marketing. BBBC is strictly a distributor and does not publish any of the books it sells. In anticipation of using database marketing, BBBC made a strategic decision right from the start to build and maintain a detailed database about its members containing all the relevant information about them. Readers fill out an insert and return it to BBBC, which then enters the data into the database. The company currently has a database of 500,000 readers and sends out a mailing about once a month.

BBBC is exploring whether to use new predictive modeling approaches to improve the efficacy of its direct mail program. For a recent mailing, the company selected 20,000 customers in Pennsylvania, New York, and Ohio from its database and included with their regular mailing a specially produced brochure for the book *The Art History of Florence*. This resulted in a 9.03 percent response rate (1806 orders) for the purchase of the book. BBBC then developed a database to calibrate a response model to identify the factors that influenced these purchases.

Each record in the database consists of two rows of data, one for each of the two choice options: purchase and no purchase. BBBC selected a number of variables that it thought might explain the observed choice behavior. Suppose that a particular customer purchased the book. The first row would then consist of a "1" to indicate choice (dependent variable) followed by the values of independent variables that could influence that choice (see below). The second row then indicates the data values associated with nonpurchase ("0"), followed by the reference data values (set to zero) for all the independent variables. On the other hand, if the customer did not purchase the book, the second row would contain the reference data values (also set to zero) associated with purchase. Data must be structured in this way to properly set up the database for logit analysis.

For purposes of analysis, we will use a subset of the database available to BBBC. It consists of 400 customers who purchased the book and 1200 who did not, thereby over-representing the "response group." Here is a description of the variables used for the analysis:

Choice: Whether the customer purchased *The Art History of Florence*. 1 corresponds to a purchase and 0 corresponds to a nonpurchase.

Gender: 0 = Female and 1 = Male

Amount_purchased: Total money spent on BBBC books

Frequency: Total number of purchases in the chosen period (used as a proxy for frequency)

Last_purchase (recency of purchase): Months since last purchase

First_purchase: Months since first purchase

P_Child: Number of children's books purchased

P_Youth: Number of youth books purchased

P_Cook: Number of cookbooks purchased

P_DIY: Number of do-it-yourself books purchased.

P_Art: Number of art books purchased

EXERCISES

BBBC currently uses a "scoring model" based on the traditional industry approach called Recency, Frequency, and Monetary (RFM) model. Briefly, it works as follows: Every customer is assigned a score based on how recently that customer purchased from the company, how frequently the customer purchases, and the total amount that customer has spent since records were kept. (This model can be implemented within Microsoft Excel using "Nested If" functions.)

Recency:
Last purchased in the last 3 months: 25 points
Last purchased in the past 3 to 6 months: 20 points
Last purchased in the past 6 to 12 months: 10 points
Last purchased in the past 12 to 18 months: 5 points
Did not purchase in the last 18 months: 0 points

Frequency (based on total purchases as recorded in the database:
Has purchased a total of less than 10 books: 10 points
Has purchased a total of 11 to 20 books: 20 points
Has purchased a total of 21 to 30 books: 30 points
Has purchased a total of 31 to 40 books: 40 points
Has purchased a total of more than 40 books: 50 points

Monetary:
Has purchased less than a total of $50: 10 points
Has purchased between $51 and $150: 20 points
Has purchased between $151 and $250: 30 points
Has purchased between $251 and $350: 40 points
Has purchased more than $350: 50 points

Total RFM score for a customer = score for Recency + score for Frequency + score for Monetary.

A consultant hired by the company recommended that BBBC try more "sophisticated" models to improve the profitability of its direct mail programs. The company is now considering two additional modeling methods, namely, an ordinary linear regression model and a binary logit model. It decided to evaluate these three models on a test mailing for *The Art History of Florence*.

1. Summarize the results of your analysis for all three models. Develop your models using the following data files, all of which contain the same data in different formats.

   - Linear regression: BBBC.XLS—1600 observations for model development.

   - Binary logit model: BBBC.DAT—1600 observations (3200 rows) for model development.

   - In addition, the file BBBCPRED.XLS contains 2300 observations for holdout prediction using the coefficients of the linear regression and binary logit models.

2. Interpret the results of these models. In particular, highlight which factors most influenced customers' decision to buy or not to buy the book.

3. Bookbinders is considering a similar mail campaign in the Midwest where they have data for 50,000 customers. Such mailings typically promote several books. The allocated cost of the mailing is $0.65/addressee (including postage) for the art book, and the book costs Bookbinders $15 to purchase and mail. The company allocates overhead to each book at 45 percent of cost. The selling price of the book is $31.95. Based on the model, which customers should Bookbinders target? How much more profit would you expect the company to generate using these models as compared to sending the mail offer to the entire list?

4. Based on the insights you gained from this modeling exercise, summarize the advantages and limitations of each of the modeling approaches. Look at both similar and dissimilar results.

5. As part of your recommendations to the company, indicate whether it should invest in developing expertise in either of the proposed new methods to develop an in-house capability to evaluate its direct mail campaigns.

6. How would you simplify and automate your recommended method(s) for future modeling efforts at the company.

APPENDIX
Regression in Excel

As a point of comparison for the logit model, run the BBBC data using ordinary least squares regression. Open BBBC.XLS file.

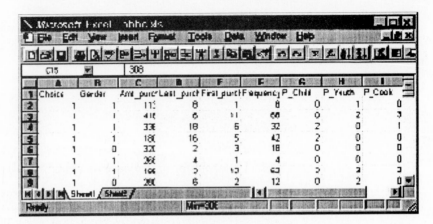

To start the regression-analysis tool, open the **Tools** menu, select **Add-Ins**, and **then Analysis ToolPak**.

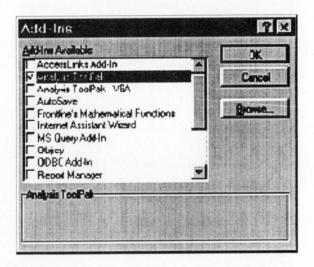

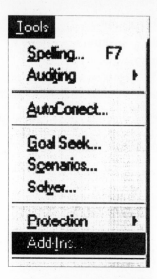

Next, from the **Tools** menu, open **Data Analysis** and select **Regression**.

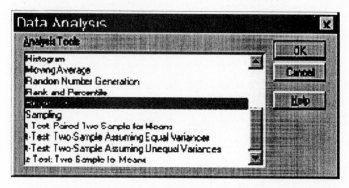

You are now all set to conduct regression analysis. Specify the regression model, as shown in the screen below.

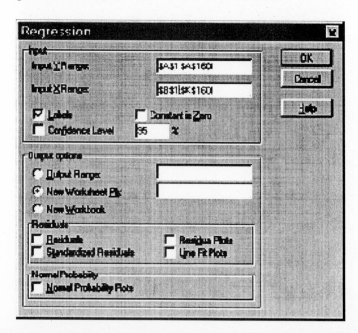

After the model runs, you should get regression results similar to those shown in the screen below:

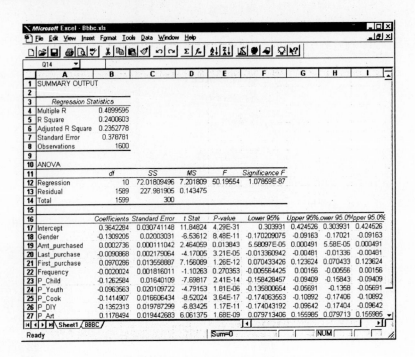

Microsoft Excel - Bbbc.xls								
File Edit View Insert Format Tools Data Window Help								

Q14								
	A	**B**	**C**	**D**	**E**	**F**	**G**	**H**	**I**

	A	B	C	D	E	F	G	H	I
1	SUMMARY OUTPUT								
2									
3	*Regression Statistics*								
4	Multiple R	0.4899595							
5	R Square	0.2400603							
6	Adjusted R Square	0.2352778							
7	Standard Error	0.378781							
8	Observations	1600							
9									
10	ANOVA								
11		*df*	*SS*	*MS*	*F*	*Significance F*			
12	Regression	10	72.01809496	7.201809	50.19554	1.07859E-87			
13	Residual	1589	227.981905	0.143475					
14	Total	1599	300						
15									
16		*Coefficients*	*Standard Error*	*t Stat*	*P-value*	*Lower 95%*	*Upper 95%*	*Lower 95.0%*	*Upper 95.0%*
17	Intercept	0.3642284	0.030741148	11.84824	4.29E-31	0.303931	0.424526	0.303931	0.424526
18	Gender	-0.1309205	0.02003031	-6.53612	8.48E-11	-0.170209075	-0.09163	-0.17021	-0.09163
19	Amt_purchased	0.0002736	0.000111042	2.464059	0.013843	5.58097E-05	0.000491	5.58E-05	0.000491
20	Last_purchase	-0.0090868	0.002179064	-4.17005	3.21E-05	-0.013360942	-0.00481	-0.01336	-0.00481
21	First_purchase	0.0970286	0.013558887	7.156089	1.26E-12	0.070433426	0.123624	0.070433	0.123624
22	Frequency	-0.0020024	0.001816011	-1.10263	0.270353	-0.005564425	0.00156	-0.00556	0.00156
23	P_Child	-0.1262584	0.01640109	-7.69817	2.41E-14	-0.158428457	-0.09409	-0.15843	-0.09409
24	P_Youth	-0.0963563	0.020109722	-4.79153	1.81E-06	-0.135800654	-0.05691	-0.1358	-0.05691
25	P_Cook	-0.1414907	0.016606434	-8.52024	3.64E-17	-0.174063553	-0.10892	-0.17406	-0.10892
26	P_DIY	-0.1352313	0.019787299	-6.83425	1.17E-11	-0.174043192	-0.09642	-0.17404	-0.09642
27	P_Art	0.1176494	0.019442683	6.061375	1.68E-09	0.079713406	0.155985	0.079713	0.155985

Sheet1 BBBC							
Ready			Sum=0			NUM	

Chapter 3

TUTORIAL FOR POSITIONING ANALYSIS

Concept

There are three broad concepts associated with this tutorial: Differentiation, Positioning, and Mapping. **Differentiation** is the creation of tangible or intangible differences on one or two key dimensions between a focal product and its main competitors. **Positioning** refers to the set of strategies organizations develop and implement to ensure that these differences occupy a distinct and important position in the minds of customers. Thus, Kentucky Fried Chicken differentiates its chicken products by using a unique blend of spices, cooking vessels, and cooking processes and positions its products as "finger-lickin' good." **Mapping** refers to techniques that enable managers to develop differentiation and positioning strategies by helping them to visualize the competitive structure of their markets as perceived by their customers. Typically, data for mapping are customer perceptions of existing products (and new concepts) along various attributes, perceptions of similarities between brands, customer preferences for products, or measures of behavioral response of customers toward the products (e.g., current market shares of the products).

Maps generated by this software are spatial representations in Euclidean space that have the following characteristics: (1) The pairwise distances between product alternatives directly indicate the "perceived similarities" between any pair of products, i.e., how close or far apart the products are in the minds of customers. (2) A vector on the map (shown by a blue or red line) indicates both magnitude and direction in the Euclidean space. The length of a vector indicates its magnitude. A blue vector geometrically denotes product attributes (i.e., direction in which the labeled attribute corresponding to a vector is increasing) and a red vector denotes the direction in which an individual's preferences are increasing. (3) The axes of the map are a special set of vectors that could represent the underlying dimensions that best characterize how customers differentiate between alternatives. One way to interpret the axes is to look for attributes that are most closely correlated with each axis. The smaller the angle between an axis and an attribute, the higher is the correlation.

This software implements the MDPREF perceptual mapping model, which is based on a factor-analytic procedure. In addition, the software implements PREFMAP-3, which enables users to introduce for each respondent a preference-vector onto a given perceptual map. Typically, a perceptual map is derived from the averaged perception data from a target segment, whereas the preference map is derived from individual-level preference data. This two-step procedure, referred to as joint-space mapping with external analysis, is based on the assumption that a target segment has a common set of perceptions among the choice alternatives, but each respondent has different preferences for those alternatives. For example, Volvo may be perceived to be a safe car by all respondents, but only some respondents may have high preference for Volvo.

(Note: All the procedures in this software are based on "vector" methods. Thus, we do not include "ideal-point" or unfolding models.)

Software

The following example illustrates the use of mapping for developing a positioning strategy for Infiniti G20. We describe the data in detail in the exercise.

From the **Model** menu, select **Positioning Analysis**. You will be prompted for a data file. For this example, select the file called G20.DAT. If you enter your own data sets, make sure that the columns are the products (or alternatives to be evaluated) and the rows contain the attribute evaluations of the products.

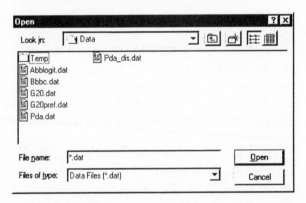

After the file loads, you will see the following split-screen window:

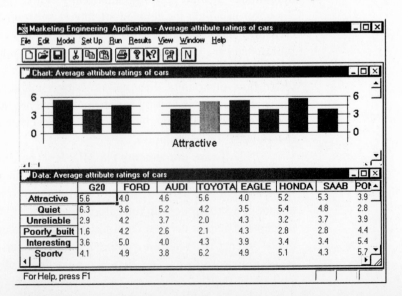

NOTE: *If you make changes to the data to evaluate alternative solutions, the program will not automatically save these changes. To save the changes (under a separate file if necessary) go to the **File** menu and click **Save As**.*

On the **Set Up** menu, click **Setup** to select the parameters for the run.

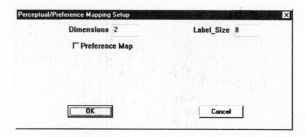

Number of dimensions: Enter either 2 or 3. If you choose a three-dimensional map, the program will produce three two-dimensional maps (Dim 1 with Dim 2; Dim1 with Dim 3, and Dim2 with Dim3).

Label Size: Because long labels might clutter the map(s), you can control the length of labels in the map by specifying between one and 10 characters.

Perceptual Map: This is the default option. For input it relies on customers' average perceptions of a set of alternatives on a set of attributes. For this exercise the data is contained in the file G20.DAT. Although this default option generates only perceptual maps and not joint-space maps (containing both perceptions and preferences), you can still obtain simple joint-space maps by including the average preference ratings in your input data matrix.

Preference Map: Select the preference map option if you have a separate file containing information on the preferences of each customer for the selected products. For the G20 exercise, the preference data are contained in the file called G20PREF.DAT. If you choose **Preference Map** you will be prompted to provide this file name.

To run the program, go to the **Run** menu and click **Run Model**.

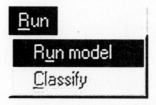

When the program is successfully executed, you will see the following map on the top part of your screen.

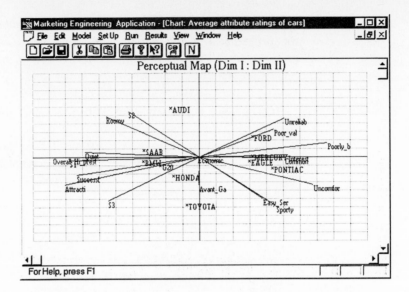

In the map, the length of an attribute vector is proportional to the variance of that attribute explained by the map.

Go to the **View** menu to find commands to customize the display. You have the following choices:

1. ***Zooming in and out***: Use the Zoom command to enlarge any portion of the display. First click **Zoom In**, and then place the cursor anywhere on the map and click. To zoom out again, go back to the **View** menu and click **Zoom Out**.

2. ***Customize the display***: On the **View** menu, click **View Options** to customize the display:

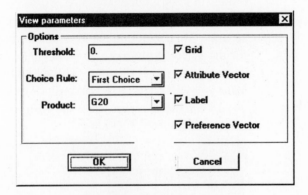

- Turn the grid on or off.
- Turn the display of attribute vectors on or off.
- Display only attributes whose variance recovery is higher than a specified number. Select the threshold values from 0 (default) to 1.0.
- If you choose to turn off the display of both attribute vectors and labels, the program will display only objects (cars in the example).

The remaining options are used with preference maps, which we describe later.

3. ***Add labels anywhere on the map***: This may be useful for future identification of the map. Click anywhere on the map, and a label dialog box will appear. Anything you enter in this dialog box will be inserted at the selected location on the map. To delete the labels you entered, go to the **Edit** menu and choose **Delete Labels**.

To print a copy of the map on an attached printer, go to the **File** menu and click **Print**. To cut and paste the map into a Windows application (e.g., Word for Windows), bring the map to the foreground, go to the **Edit** menu and select **Cut** or **Copy** and then bring a Windows application to the foreground, go to the **Edit** menu, and select **Paste**.

In the case of 3-D maps, the program displays automatically only a map of dimensions 1 and 2. To view the other dimensions on the **Results** menu, choose **Summary** and then **View Next Chart** as shown below.

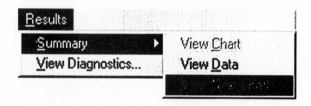

Alternatively, click on the button on the Menu Bar to view the next chart.

Preference maps

If you chose **Preference Map** in the **Setup** menu, the map will include the preference vectors of each individual shown as red lines. The length of a preference vector is proportional to the variance of that respondent's preferences that are explained by the map.

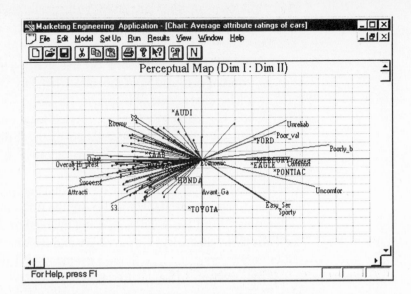

Customize the viewing and analysis options: As with the perceptual map, you can use the options under the **View** menu to customize the display. You will have some new options that were not available with perceptual maps. Go to **View** and choose **View Options.** You can use these options to:

- Turn the display of the preference vectors on or off.
- Select a product whose market share you would like to explore at various locations on the map.
- Select the choice rule to be used for market-share computations. Under the first-choice rule, we assume that each customer will purchase only his or her most preferred product. Under the share-of-preference rule, we assume that the probability that a customer will select a product is proportional to the product's share of preference with respect to all the products included in the model.

NOTE: *The share-of-preference model, as implemented here, arbitrarily sets the preference value of a customer's least preferred product to 0.*

To compute an index of market share at any location on the map for a selected product, place the cursor anywhere on the map and click the **right mouse button**. Cross hairs will appear at that position on the map, along with a market-share figure (at the bottom of the screen) as shown below. It is best to interpret the computed market share as a measure of the *relative attractiveness* (relative to market share at the original position) of the selected location on the map for the selected product, rather than as an indicator of the absolute magnitude of the market share that will be realized.

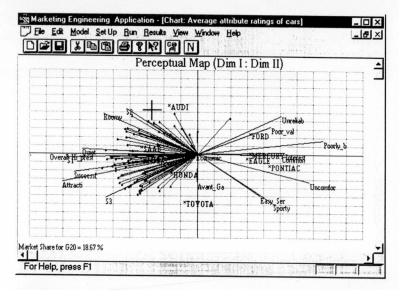

NOTE: *In computing market share, we assume that the selected product is relocated to the new position shown by the cross hairs (the map will still show the selected product at its original location for purposes of comparison), while all other products remain at their original positions.*

To view additional information of a diagnostic nature, go to the **Results** menu and select **View Diagnostics**. This produces a display of additional information useful in evaluating the statistical adequacy of the generated map. You can print this information to an attached printer by going to the **File** menu and selecting **Print**, or use the Windows cut-and-paste option to copy this information into another Windows application, such as Word for Windows, for further editing.

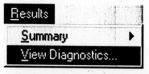

Marketing Engineering Application - [Diagnostic: Average attribute ratings of cars]

File Edit Model Set Up Run Results View Window Help

Diagnostics for Perceptual Map

Total variance accounted for by the 2 dimensions: .729
Cumulative proportion of variance accounted for by each dimension:

1	2	3	4	5	6	7	8	9	10
.542	.729	.841	.914	.943	.966	.986	.996	1.000	1.000

The following table summarizes the variance explained for each
attribute/object in the 2-dimensional map you requested.

Attribute/Object	Mean	Variance	Variance explained
Attractive	4.780	.737	.968
Quiet	4.410	1.050	.768
Unreliable	3.420	.755	.759
Poorly_built	3.090	1.056	.868

. . . .

For Help, press F1

If you had checked **Preference Map** in the **Set Up** menu, you will get additional diagnostics as shown in the screen below:

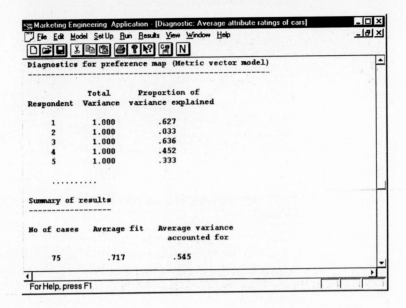

References

Green, Paul E. and Wind, Yoram 1973, *Multiattribute Decisions in Marketing: A Measurement Approach*, The Dryden Press, Hinsdale, Illinois.

Green, Paul E.; Carmone, Frank J., Jr.; and Smith, Scott M. 1989, *Multidimensional Scaling: Concepts and Application*, Allyn and Bacon, Boston, Massachusetts.

Muelman, Jacqueline; Heiser, Wilhelm; and Carroll, J. Douglas 1986, *PREFMAP-3 User's Guide*, Bell Laboratories, Murray Hill, New Jersey 07974.

POSITIONING THE INFINITI G20 CASE*

Introducing the G20

In April 1990, Nissan's Infiniti division planned to introduce the G20 in the U.S., adding a third model to the existing Infiniti line. The G20 was already available in Europe and Japan under the name Primera. The car, equipped with a four-cylinder engine developing 140 horsepower, would be Infiniti's entry-level luxury car. Initial market response to the G20 in the U.S. was disappointing, and management wondered how it might retarget or reposition the car to improve its market performance.

Background

In 1989, three years after Honda first introduced its Acura line, Toyota and Nissan attacked the U.S. luxury car market, a segment previously dominated by American and German manufacturers.

In November 1989, Nissan launched its new luxury Infiniti division with the $40,000 Q45 as its lead car and the $20,000 M30. However Nissan was somewhat late: In August 1989, three months before Nissan shipped its first Infiniti, Toyota had introduced Lexus, its luxury brand with a two-car line comprising the $40,000 LS400 and the entry-level LS250.

As the figures for January to September 1990 showed, Lexus outsold Infiniti by 50,000 to 15,000. The reasons for Infiniti's slow start were threefold.

- First the Infiniti Q45 came to the market after the Lexus LS400 had established a good market position.
- Second Lexus had two very good cars, whereas Infiniti's M30 coupe received poor evaluations from the automobile press and from customers.
- Finally the eccentric Infiniti advertising campaign that showed scenes of nature, but not the car itself, shared some of the blame. ("Infiniti may not be doing so well, but, hey, at least sales of rocks and trees are skyrocketing," commented comedian Jay Leno.)

Research data

Exhibits 1–4 summarize some of the data that Infiniti had in early 1990. Data in Exhibits 1 and 2 are based on a survey of customers from its target segments, described as people between 25 and 35 with annual

---

* This case was developed by Katrin Starke and Arvind Rangaswamy and describes a real situation using hypothetical data.

household incomes between $50,000 and $100,000 (when the survey was administered, the Lexus LS250 was not yet well known to the respondents to be included in the study). The three sub-segments in Exhibit 1 (denoted S1, S2, and S3) are based on information provided by Infiniti managers. Exhibit 3 is derived from sales brochures describing the characteristics of each car. Exhibit 4 summarizes demographic and psychographic information about the three sub-segments and was compiled from databases supplied by Claritas, Inc.

	G20	Ford T-bird	Audi 90	Toyota Supra	Eagle Talon	Honda Prelude	Saab 900	Pontiac Firebird	BMW 318i	Mercury Capri
Attractive	5.6	4.0	4.6	5.6	4.0	5.2	5.3	3.9	5.7	3.9
Quiet	6.3	3.6	5.2	4.2	3.5	5.4	4.8	2.8	5.0	3.3
Unreliable	2.9	4.2	3.7	2.0	4.3	3.2	3.7	3.9	2.3	4.0
Poorly Built	1.6	4.2	2.6	2.1	4.3	2.8	2.8	4.4	1.8	4.3
Interesting	3.6	5.0	4.0	4.3	3.9	3.4	3.4	5.4	3.3	3.9
Sporty	4.1	4.9	3.8	6.2	4.9	5.1	4.3	5.7	4.1	5.2
Uncomfortable	2.4	4.0	2.4	3.7	4.0	3.3	2.8	4.3	3.5	4.4
Roomy	5.6	3.9	5.3	3.5	3.6	3.9	5.1	3.3	4.3	3.6
Easy Service	4.6	4.9	3.5	4.9	4.6	5.0	3.8	4.7	4.1	4.6
High Prestige	5.4	3.5	5.6	5.3	2.8	4.7	5.7	3.8	6.4	3.3
Common	3.5	3.6	3.4	2.9	4.3	3.9	1.9	4.3	2.8	3.9
Economical	3.6	3.7	3.6	3.2	4.9	5.0	4.3	3.1	4.3	4.6
Successful	5.3	4.2	5.0	5.5	3.7	5.6	5.3	4.4	5.9	3.9
Avant-garde	4.3	3.6	3.6	4.9	4.4	3.9	4.7	4.1	3.7	4.5
Poor Value	3.4	4.3	4.3	3.5	3.6	2.6	2.9	4.3	3.3	3.8
Preferences										
Overall	6.3	3.9	6.0	5.5	4.0	6.5	6.8	3.0	6.7	4.0
Segment I (S1)	4.3	2.1	6.0	6.1	3.3	6.0	7.5	1.2	8.3	1.7
Segment II (S2)	5.9	6.0	7.7	3.5	3.1	5.5	5.4	2.5	5.4	5.8
Segment III (S3)	8.4	2.1	3.4	8.1	5.8	8.3	8.4	5.3	7.3	3.4

EXHIBIT 1
Survey results with average perception and average preference ratings on a scale from 1 to 9 (G20.DAT).

EXHIBIT 2
Individual-level preference data, measured on a scale from 1 to 9, with
higher numbers representing increased preference (GEOPREF.DAT).

	G20	Ford T-bird	Audi 90	Toyota Supra	Eagle Talon	Honda Prelude	Saab 900	Pontiac Firebird	BMW 318i	Mercury Capri
1	4.0	7.0	8.0	3.0	4.0	5.0	5.0	1.0	4.0	5.0
2	4.0	8.0	6.0	5.0	8.0	7.0	3.0	1.0	5.0	2.0
3	8.0	5.0	9.0	4.0	1.0	7.0	7.0	2.0	4.0	4.0
4	7.0	1.0	8.0	1.0	4.0	6.0	5.0	5.0	7.0	3.0
5	8.0	8.0	8.0	3.0	5.0	4.0	3.0	2.0	8.0	6.0
6	5.0	6.0	5.0	5.0	2.0	4.0	8.0	4.0	4.0	7.0
7	3.0	9.0	7.0	4.0	4.0	3.0	6.0	4.0	3.0	6.0
8	4.0	7.0	9.0	3.0	1.0	7.0	9.0	3.0	6.0	6.0
9	8.0	6.0	6.0	4.0	5.0	5.0	1.0	2.0	8.0	7.0
10	6.0	4.0	6.0	3.0	2.0	8.0	7.0	3.0	1.0	8.0
11	8.0	6.0	8.0	4.0	6.0	8.0	7.0	1.0	2.0	7.0
12	8.0	5.0	6.0	6.0	2.0	3.0	8.0	1.0	6.0	6.0
13	4.0	2.0	9.0	4.0	1.0	5.0	5.0	4.0	8.0	5.0
14	5.0	5.0	8.0	5.0	6.0	4.0	6.0	1.0	3.0	7.0
15	6.0	5.0	9.0	1.0	3.0	6.0	8.0	3.0	6.0	3.0
16	6.0	3.0	9.0	2.0	7.0	8.0	6.0	3.0	7.0	3.0
17	8.0	5.0	8.0	1.0	1.0	8.0	9.0	2.0	5.0	4.0
18	5.0	9.0	7.0	5.0	2.0	4.0	7.0	5.0	6.0	1.0
19	6.0	7.0	9.0	6.0	2.0	6.0	3.0	5.0	4.0	5.0
20	6.0	9.0	8.0	2.0	3.0	8.0	6.0	1.0	7.0	5.0
21	7.0	7.0	9.0	4.0	1.0	3.0	4.0	1.0	4.0	3.0
22	6.0	9.0	6.0	2.0	3.0	4.0	6.0	1.0	6.0	3.0
23	5.0	4.0	8.0	4.0	1.0	4.0	1.0	1.0	8.0	5.0
24	7.0	4.0	8.0	3.0	2.0	3.0	4.0	6.0	9.0	5.0
25	4.0	9.0	7.0	3.0	1.0	7.0	2.0	1.0	5.0	7.0
26	8.0	2.0	1.0	9.0	4.0	8.0	8.0	5.0	8.0	4.0
27	8.0	6.0	5.0	8.0	4.0	8.0	7.0	7.0	5.0	1.0
28	9.0	1.0	2.0	4.0	9.0	9.0	9.0	4.0	8.0	3.0
29	9.0	2.0	4.0	8.0	7.0	8.0	9.0	8.0	5.0	6.0
30	8.0	3.0	4.0	8.0	7.0	6.0	6.0	4.0	5.0	1.0
31	8.0	3.0	2.0	9.0	5.0	8.0	9.0	5.0	7.0	5.0
32	5.0	1.0	2.0	7.0	5.0	9.0	9.0	7.0	8.0	6.0
33	9.0	1.0	4.0	9.0	6.0	9.0	9.0	5.0	9.0	2.0
34	8.0	2.0	6.0	8.0	7.0	9.0	8.0	5.0	9.0	5.0
35	9.0	1.0	7.0	9.0	5.0	7.0	6.0	6.0	4.0	1.0
36	8.0	1.0	4.0	9.0	6.0	8.0	8.0	3.0	7.0	4.0
37	9.0	2.0	3.0	9.0	5.0	8.0	9.0	7.0	9.0	6.0
38	8.0	2.0	3.0	6.0	5.0	9.0	9.0	3.0	9.0	6.0
39	9.0	2.0	4.0	9.0	7.0	8.0	7.0	7.0	9.0	1.0
40	8.0	3.0	2.0	7.0	5.0	8.0	9.0	5.0	6.0	1.0
41	9.0	3.0	4.0	8.0	8.0	9.0	6.0	2.0	9.0	6.0
42	8.0	3.0	2.0	8.0	6.0	8.0	9.0	4.0	7.0	2.0
43	9.0	2.0	1.0	8.0	6.0	7.0	9.0	5.0	9.0	5.0
44	9.0	2.0	3.0	9.0	7.0	8.0	9.0	7.0	5.0	4.0
45	9.0	2.0	3.0	7.0	6.0	9.0	9.0	7.0	5.0	2.0
46	8.0	1.0	2.0	9.0	5.0	8.0	9.0	4.0	9.0	4.0
47	9.0	2.0	3.0	9.0	6.0	9.0	9.0	6.0	8.0	1.0
48	9.0	3.0	6.0	8.0	2.0	8.0	9.0	4.0	8.0	4.0
49	9.0	1.0	2.0	9.0	6.0	8.0	9.0	4.0	7.0	1.0

EXHIBIT 2 cont'd

Individual-level preference data, measured on a scale from 1 to 9, with higher numbers representing increased preference (GEOPREF.DAT).

	G20	Ford T-Bird	Audi 90	Toyota Supra	Eagle Talon	Honda Prelude	Saab 900	Pontiac Firebird	BMW 318i	Mercury Capri
50	9.0	3.0	6.0	9.0	6.0	9.0	8.0	8.0	7.0	5.0
51	8.0	3.0	5.0	7.0	2.0	8.0	8.0	6.0	8.0	1.0
52	9.0	5.0	4.0	7.0	1.0	2.0	5.0	1.0	9.0	3.0
53	7.0	4.0	4.0	3.0	4.0	9.0	8.0	2.0	5.0	4.0
54	7.0	2.0	6.0	5.0	3.0	7.0	6.0	4.0	8.0	6.0
55	5.0	2.0	3.0	5.0	5.0	8.0	9.0	1.0	9.0	1.0
56	4.0	5.0	6.0	5.0	4.0	9.0	8.0	4.0	6.0	4.0
57	7.0	1.0	7.0	8.0	7.0	7.0	7.0	2.0	6.0	5.0
58	5.0	3.0	3.0	7.0	2.0	8.0	7.0	2.0	9.0	6.0
59	4.0	4.0	5.0	8.0	2.0	6.0	6.0	6.0	6.0	1.0
60	8.0	4.0	9.0	4.0	5.0	5.0	5.0	2.0	7.0	4.0
61	8.0	4.0	5.0	4.0	3.0	6.0	8.0	3.0	7.0	4.0
62	7.0	5.0	7.0	7.0	6.0	6.0	6.0	5.0	7.0	3.0
63	8.0	2.0	2.0	4.0	5.0	8.0	8.0	1.0	9.0	2.0
64	5.0	6.0	4.0	7.0	4.0	4.0	5.0	1.0	8.0	1.0
65	7.0	4.0	4.0	6.0	5.0	3.0	6.0	1.0	6.0	4.0
66	8.0	2.0	9.0	3.0	5.0	7.0	8.0	4.0	6.0	2.0
67	3.0	5.0	8.0	7.0	6.0	3.0	8.0	2.0	9.0	6.0
68	6.0	1.0	3.0	5.0	2.0	9.0	7.0	2.0	6.0	5.0
69	6.0	3.0	8.0	8.0	5.0	8.0	6.0	3.0	3.0	1.0
70	7.0	2.0	8.0	8.0	3.0	9.0	7.0	4.0	4.0	5.0
71	7.0	1.0	7.0	7.0	8.0	8.0	9.0	1.0	9.0	1.0
72	6.0	5.0	5.0	5.0	4.0	6.0	9.0	4.0	8.0	2.0
73	7.0	5.0	4.0	4.0	2.0	6.0	8.0	5.0	9.0	5.0
74	8.0	5.0	6.0	6.0	6.0	7.0	7.0	4.0	8.0	4.0
75	7.0	3.0	6.0	8.0	4.0	7.0	7.0	5.0	5.0	3.0

	G20	Ford T-bird	Audi 90	Toyota Supra	Eagle Talon	Honda Prelude	Saab 900	Pontiac Firebird	BMW 318i	Mercury Capri
Base Price ($)	17,500	15,783	20,200	23,280	16,437	14,945	18,295	12,690	19,900	13,500
Length (Inches)	175	198.7	176	181.9	170.5	175.6	184.5	192.0	170.3	166.1
Width (Inches)	66.7	72.7	67.6	68.7	66.7	67.3	66.5	72.4	64.8	64.6
Height (Inches)	54.9	52.7	54.3	51.2	51.4	29.2	56.1	49.8	53.5	50.2
Curb Weight (lbs.)	2,535	3,600	3,170	3,535	3,100	2,740	2,825	3,485	2,600	2,487
Fuel Economy (Mpg) City	24	17	18	17	20	23	20	16	22	23
Highway	32	24	24	22	25	27	26	24	27	28
Horspower, SAE.net (Bhp)	140@ 6,400 rpm	210@ 4,000 rpm	164@ 6,000 rpm	232@ 5,600 rpm	195@ 6,000 rpm	135@ 6,200 rpm	140@ 6,000 rpm	240@ 4,400 rpm	134@ 6,000 rpm	132@ 6,000 rpm
Warranty, Years/Miles, Bumper-to-Bumper	4/ 60,000	1/ 12,000	3/ 50,000	3/ 36,000	1/ 12,000	3/ 36,000	3/ 36,000	3/ 50,000	3/ 36,000	1/ 12,000

EXHIBIT 3
Some physical characteristics of the cars.

Segment Characteristic	Segment I (Western Yuppie, Single)	Segment II (Upwardly Mobile Families)	Segment III (American Dreamers)
Segment Size	(25%)	(45%)	(30%)
Education	College Grads	College Grads or Some College	College Grads or Some College
Predominant Employment	Professionals	White-Collar	White-Collar
Age Group	25-35	25-35	25-35
Predominant Ethnic Background	White	White	Mix (Asian, White)
Average Household Income	$81,000	$68,000	$59,000
Persons per Household	1.42	3.8	2.4
Percent Married	32%	75%	55%
Watch Late Night TV	27%	9%	17%
Watch Daytime TV	3%	45%	5%
Read Computer Magazines	39%	6%	10%
Read Business Magazines	58%	23%	27%
Read Entertainment Magazines	3%	14%	30%
Read Infant and Parenting Magazines	1%	17%	2%
Rent Movies	43%	85%	38%
Possess an American Express Card	48%	45%	75%
Own Investment Funds	24%	18%	47%
Go Fishing	2%	30%	3%
Sail, Scuba Dive or Ski	49%	2%	20%

EXHIBIT 4
Data about the sub-segments.

EXERCISES

1. Describe the two (or, if applicable, three) dimensions underlying the perceptual maps that you generated. Based on these maps, how do people in this market perceive the Infiniti G20 compared with its competitors?

2. Infiniti promoted the G20 as a Japanese car (basic version $17,500) with a German feel, basically a car that was like the BMW 318i ($20,000), but lower priced. Is this a credible claim, given the perceptions and preferences of the respondents?

3. Which attributes are most important in influencing preference for these cars in the three segments (S1, S2, and S3) shown on these maps? To which segment(s) would you market the Infiniti G20? How would you reposition the Infiniti G20 to best suit the chosen segment(s)? Briefly describe the marketing program you would use to target the chosen segment(s).

4. What ongoing research program would you recommend to Infiniti to improve its evaluation of its segmentation of the market and positioning of its G20?

5. Summarize the advantages and limitations of the software provided for this application.

POSITIONING THE ConneCtor EXERCISE

(This exercise is a follow-up to Conglomerate Inc's new PDA Case)

Background

Following the preliminary findings of their market research study, Conglomerate Inc. hired LR Inc. to help them position their new product in a specific target market segment that they tentatively called "Hard Hats." (Construction and emergency workers, primarily.)

LR Inc. reviewed the key product features that appeared to differentiate ConneCtor from its major competitors and identified the following dimensions.

Instant communication from PDA to PDA
Connectivity
Cellular phone and pager, fax and email
Calendar, scheduler, calculator and address book
Open system
Paperless note pad
Voice recognition

LR then ran two focus groups among "Hard Hats" and determined that the features that seemed to interest the groups the most were connectivity and communication. After careful discussion with Conglomerate's Ad Agency, they agreed to develop and test an ad campaign around the feature, "communication."

To test the potential effectiveness of the ad, LR recruited 75 "Hard Hats" who were given advertisements and descriptions of product features for the New PDA as well as for the following competing brands:

Sharp_5800
Sony_PIC2000
Newton_130
Hitachi
HP_200LX
Pilot_5000
Canon
Psion_3c
NEC_Pro

Respondents were then asked two sets of questions:

First, each respondent was asked to evaluate each of the brands (including the New PDA) along a 1 to 7 scale (where 1 = Worst and 7 = Best) along the following dimensions:

Good_value
Light
Reliable
Large
Ease of service
Expandability
Screen quality
Easy to use
Shows I am successful
Common brand
Economical
Permits connectivity
Permits communication
Permits effective use of spreadsheet

These data are available in a file called pdaperc.dat.

Next, each of the 75 respondents was asked to provide preference scores from 1 (like the least) to 10 (like the most) for each of the brands at their suggested retail prices. These data are available in a file called pdapref.dat.

LR was then asked to use perceptual mapping to evaluate the effectiveness of the Positioning for the New PDA.

EXERCISES

1. Describe the two (or if applicable, three) dimensions underlying the perceptual maps that you generate. Based on those maps, how do "Hard Hats" perceive ConneCtor compared with its competitors?

2. Run the analysis with the preference data. What dimensions seem to drive choice and likely market share in this market? (*Be sure to select "New PDA" when viewing the map—and remember that the right mouse button gives market share estimates.*)

3. How would you modify the ad campaign for the ConneCtor to better position it to this target segment?

4. What program of research would you recommend to refine your findings?

5. Comment on the advantages and disadvantages of the perceptual mapping approach to product positioning.

Chapter 4

TUTORIAL FOR CONJOINT ANALYSIS

Concept

Conjoint Analysis is widely employed for designing new products. It is a procedure for measuring, analyzing, and predicting customers' responses to new products and to new features of existing products. It enables companies to decompose customers' preferences for products and services (provided as descriptions or visual images) into "part-worth" utilities associated with each option of each attribute or feature of the product. They can then recombine the part worths to predict customers' preferences for any product that can be developed using the attributes and options included in the study. They can use this procedure to determine the optimal product concept or to identify market segments that value a particular product concept highly.

Software

On the **Model** menu, select **Conjoint Analysis**. You will see the following window:

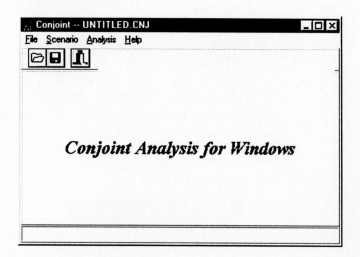

Using the **File** menu you can **Open** an existing conjoint analysis file (if you have one). For the Forte Hotel design exercise, open file hotel.cnj. Otherwise, proceed to the **Scenario** menu. You can also **Save** information from a session to a file and retrieve it later.

The tutorial consists of three sections: (1) Designing a conjoint study, (2) Obtaining data about customer preferences, and (3) Conducting market simulations. For the Forte Hotel Design exercise, we have already completed the design and data collection stages.

Designing a conjoint study

The first step in designing a conjoint study is to generate a scenario by specifying the product attributes and their possible options. To do this you perform three substeps.

1. Identify the major attributes of the product category of interest. For example, "Leisure activities available to patrons" could be a major attribute in designing a new hotel.

   ■ Identify attributes by asking experts, surveying consumers or conducting focus groups. Attributes can be structural characteristics, product features or options, appearance of product, or even marketing-mix variables, such as price.
   ■ Omit from the analysis attributes on which all products and new product concepts are similar. For example, if all hotels offer express check-out and that service is considered essential in all new hotels, you can omit it from the study. It is also important to use attributes that customers in the target segment care about.

   On the **Scenario** menu, select **Edit Attributes and Levels**:

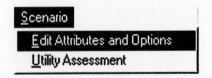

   You will see the following screen:

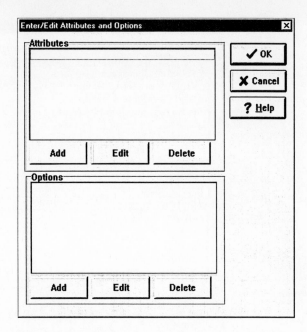

Click the **Add** button under **Attributes** to specify the product or service attributes of interest in the study. You can add up to six attributes. You can edit a previously entered attribute by clicking **Edit**. You can also **Delete** any attribute entered.

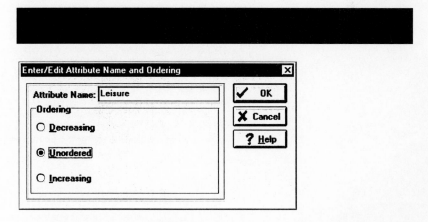

You can use the **Ordering** option to specify whether preferences will be decreasing, unordered, or increasing with respect to levels of this attribute. This educational version permits only the unordered option.

2. Once you have entered your list of attributes, you must enter at least two options of each attribute that are available, as shown in the example below for the attribute Leisure. Use the **Add** button to list levels. You should choose the major options already available in the market, as well as new options being considered for the proposed new product. Use the arrow keys or the mouse to select the attributes for which you want to **Add** the appropriate levels.

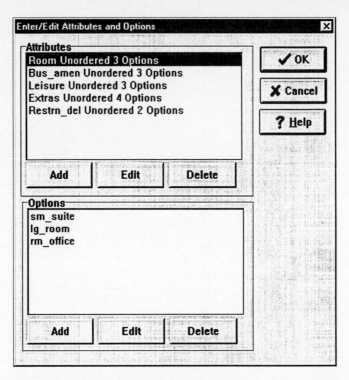

3. To generate a set of products for customer evaluation, describe each product as a combination of attribute options. After you have entered all the attributes and attribute options, click **OK**. You will see the following screen:

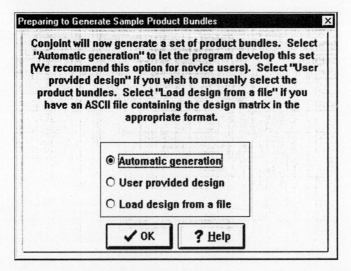

Automatic generation produces a set of orthogonal product profiles. Unless you are experienced in conjoint analysis, select **Automatic Generation** (the default option). If you select this option, the program generates a subset of products from the total set of products containing all possible combinations of attribute options. The selected subset is such that it ensures that every option of every attribute is present in a sufficient number of products to allow for the proper estimation of the importance of that attribute option to a consumer.

Knowledgeable users can select their own subsets of products using criteria other than orthogonality. You can specify a set of product profiles for analysis by choosing **User-Provided Design**. The program will then display a list of packages that it selected automatically. You can use this list as a starting point for designing your own set of packages.

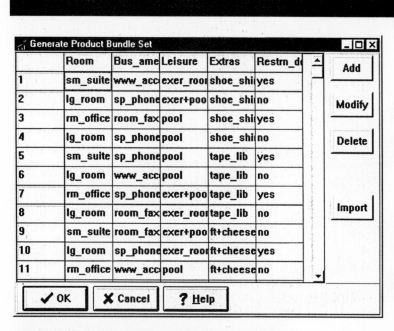

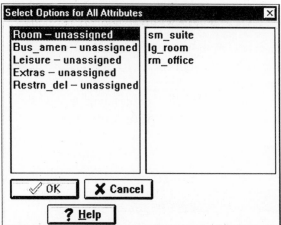

You can also choose **Load Design from File** to load your own design matrix from an external ASCII text file. An example file for a five-attribute design matrix is shown below:

```
0 0 0 0 0
1 1 2 0 1
2 2 1 0 0
1 1 1 0 1
0 1 1 1 0
1 0 1 1 1
2 1 2 1 0
1 2 0 1 1
0 2 2 2 1
1 1 0 2 0
2 0 1 2 1
1 1 1 2 0
0 1 1 3 1
1 2 1 3 0
2 1 0 3 1
1 0 2 3 0
```

In specifying a design matrix, follow the convention for labeling attribute options shown in the example above: Attribute 1 (the first column) has three options labeled 0, 1, and 2; Attribute 5 has two options labeled 0 and 1.

For this tutorial, we have already specified a design matrix, completing section 1. For the rest of this tutorial, we will use this predefined example. If you have not already done so, go to the **File** menu and click **Open** to load the hotel.cnj file.

Assessing preferences of customers

In this section, we demonstrate how to obtain respondent evaluations for the selected products. For purposes of illustration, you will be the respondent.

Begin the utility assessment procedure by opening the **Scenario** menu and choosing **Utility Assessment**.

You will see a dialog box requesting an ID under which your preferences will be stored for further analysis. Enter your name or a unique ID and click **OK**.

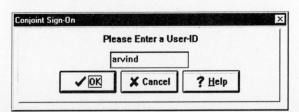

You will see the following screen:

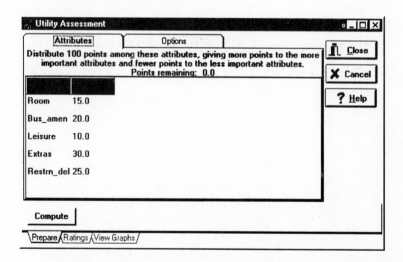

Under **Utility Assessment**, you can select either **Prepare** or **Ratings** procedures or do both in sequence.

1. ***Prepare*** *(also known as self-explicated ratings)*: To complete the "Prepare" task, you must provide information regarding (1) your relative preferences for the attributes, and (2) relative preferences for the available options of each attribute. You have 100 points to distribute across the attributes.

After you assess the importance, or weight, of each attribute, click the **Options** tab and rank the options of the Leisure attribute. Click the **Next Attrib** button to go to the next attribute, which in this case, is "Extras." After you enter your rankings for all options of all attributes, click **Compute**.

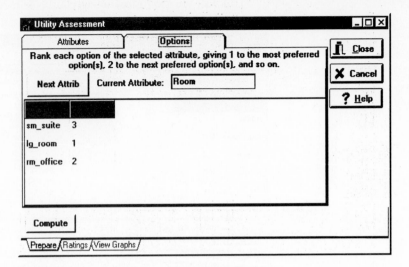

2. ***Ratings option***: Choose the ratings task by clicking the **Ratings** tab at the bottom of the screen. You will see the dialog box below:

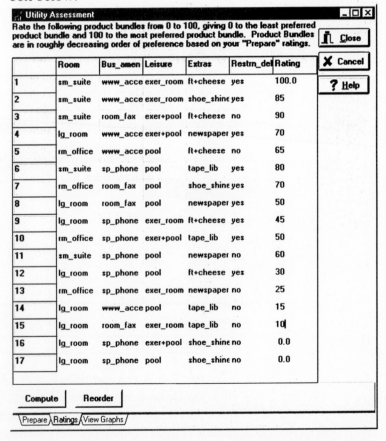

   In the "Rating" column, enter a value between 0 and 100 to reflect your preference for each of the hotel packages presented, one per row. If you complete the prepare task before selecting the ratings task, the program will already have sequenced the packages according to your Prepare ratings. The most-preferred package appears at the top with a value of 100, and the least-preferred package appears at the bottom with a value of 0. Interspersed between these two packages are a carefully selected set of alternative packages for you to evaluate. If you initiated the ratings task without completing the Prepare task, the program will list the packages in random order. Doing the Prepare task before the Ratings task makes the ratings task easier.

At any time during the ratings task, you can click **Reorder** to order the packages from most preferred to least preferred, which makes the ratings process easier:

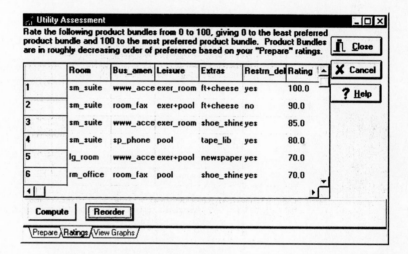

Once you have rated all the packages, click **Compute**. The program then computes the utility function corresponding to the values you provided in the "Ratings" column.

3. ***Graphics option***: Once you have finished the ratings task, click **View Graphs** to see a graphical depiction of the utility function generated using your ratings. For consistency the utility function is scaled to lie between 0 and 100 as it does in the prepare task.

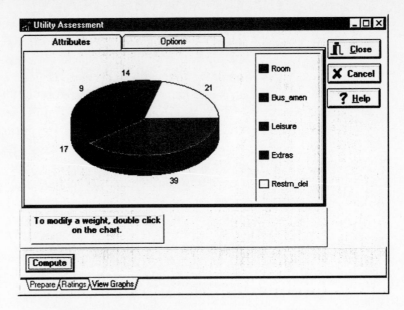

By clicking the **Options** tab, you can see a bar graph of the part-worth utilities corresponding to each option of each attribute, as shown below.

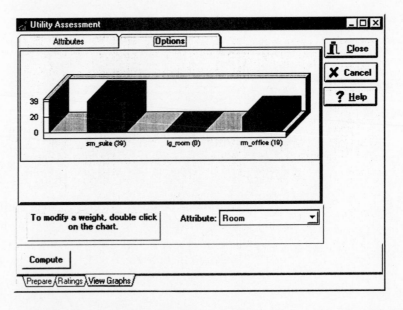

After viewing the graphs, you may think that the relative weights for attributes and attribute options shown in the graphs do not convey your true preferences. In this case, you can alter the weights assigned to any attribute or attribute option. Double-click on either the pie chart (to change part worths of attributes) or the bar graph (to change part worths of attribute options).

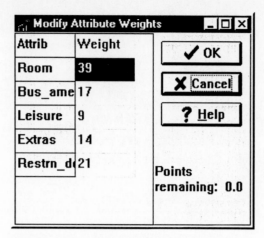

NOTE: *For consistency, attribute weights must sum to 100, and weights for attribute options must range from 0 to a maximum value corresponding to the weight given to that attribute.*

You can go back and forth between **Prepare**, **Ratings**, and **Graphs** as many times as necessary, until you are sure that the utility function shown in the graphs reflects your true preferences. When you finish this task, the program will save a copy of the final utility function under a file name that includes the ID you used to sign on. Click **Close**.

Conducting market simulations

Once you have obtained utility functions from a sample of respondents, the fun part begins. Using the program you can design new products that will be attractive to the target segment in the presence of existing products in the marketplace. The success of new products depends on how well their attribute options match customer preferences compared to the competitive offerings in the market. Go to the **Analysis** menu. You must perform the following tasks before you can evaluate new product concepts:

1. From the **Analysis** menu, choose **Load Part Worth File(s).** Select any subset of respondents for analysis using any suitable criteria. For example, you can select only male respondents for further analysis. You can then repeat the analyses for other subsegments. The program stores utility functions under the ID name of each respondent who provided the data, adding the extension .PRT to the ID name.

NOTE: *Once you have saved part-worth data in a file, you don't have to reload these files each time you run the program. For the Forte Hotel exercise, the hotel.cnj file includes the part-worth files of all 40 respondents. When you do the exercise, you can go directly to*

Create/Edit Existing Product Profiles or to other commands on the Analysis menu.

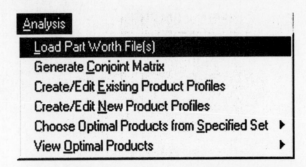

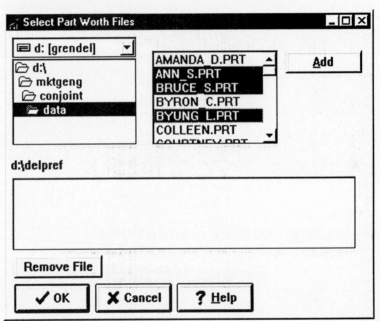

Select all the files you want to include and click **Add**. (To select multiple files at the same time, press the Ctrl key while clicking the file name). For our analysis, we will select all 40 respondents. After selecting the files, click **OK**.

2. Next load these files into the program by selecting **Generate Conjoint Matrix**, as shown below. Use the scroll bar to view sections of the matrix that are hidden from view.

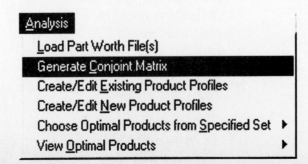

Attribs	Room			Bus_ame			Leisure		
Options	sm_suite	lg_room	rm_office	www_acc	sp_phone	room_fax	exer_roo	pool	exer+poo
THOMAS_	16.00	0.00	33.00	0.00	16.00	10.00	13.00	0.00	10.00
TIFFAN_L	14.00	0.00	30.00	7.00	0.00	19.00	20.00	10.00	0.00
TRACI_L	25.00	0.00	17.00	13.00	0.00	8.00	0.00	20.00	38.00
TREVOR_	17.00	32.00	0.00	0.00	15.00	15.00	31.00	0.00	28.00
VLADIMIR	0.00	14.00	19.00	9.00	0.00	22.00	10.00	18.00	0.00
Average	18.15	10.27	14.85	8.45	11.38	11.00	8.52	10.35	10.63

Load File   Close   ? Help

The last row of the conjoint matrix shows the average part worth of each attribute option across the selected respondents. The average part worth gives a good indication of the attribute options that are attractive to the selected group of customers. After viewing this, click **Close**.

You can also directly load an ASCII file containing the part-worth data of a number of respondents by clicking on the **Load File** button and specifying the file name. The file to be loaded should have the format described under "Load an ASCII file containing the data in the appropriate format" described in the **Introduction to Software** section of this volume. Note that if you load a new file, any previously loaded data will be removed before the new data is entered into the data matrix.

3. To specify a set of existing products against which proposed new concepts will compete, go to the **Analysis** menu and select the **Create/Edit Existing Product Profiles**.

Analysis
Load Part Worth File(s)
Generate Conjoint Matrix
Create/Edit Existing Product Profiles
Create/Edit New Product Profiles
Choose Optimal Products from Specified Set ▶
View Optimal Products ▶

You will see the following screen:

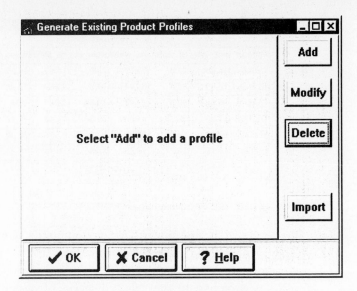

When you click **Add** or **Modify**, you will see the following screen:

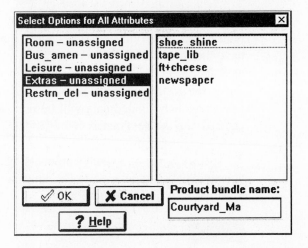

Specify each product by selecting the appropriate attribute options corresponding to that product. It is advisable to include only products that are likely to compete directly with the proposed new product concepts.

If more than one existing product has the same set of attribute options, you should define just one of them. Once you have defined a product, the screen will look as shown. You can also provide a unique name associated with this product. Here, we called this package the "Courtyard by Marriott."

After you define all existing products of interest for this analysis, click **OK**. You will see a screen similar to the following:

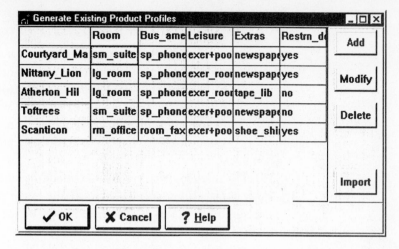

4. Next specify a set of candidate new product-concepts. (If you do not specify any new-product profiles for analysis, you can compute the estimated market shares of the existing products. This serves as a validity check of the data set.) From the **Analysis** menu, choose **Create/Edit New Product Profiles** as shown below.

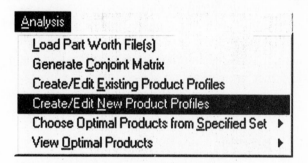

Specify the attribute options for the new product using the procedure we described earlier for creating existing product profiles.

5. By now, you have specified most of the information that Conjoint Analysis needs to simulate the market performance of the selected products. From the **Analysis** menu, click **Choose Optimal Products from Specified Set**. You will be offered three choice rules for assessing the market performance of the new products:

> ***Maximum utility rule***: Each respondent is assumed to select the product that provides the highest utility among the competing products and a specific new product concept being evaluated. Conjoint Analysis evaluates each new product concept in turn in competition with the existing products. The maximum utility rule is the preferred analysis option if customers buy products in the product category infrequently.

> ***Share of utility rule***: Each respondent's share of purchases of a particular product is considered to be a function of the utility for that product as compared to the total utility for all

products in the competitive set. This analysis option is most suitable for products customers buy frequently.

Logit choice rule: The share for each product for each respondent is considered to be a function of the "weighted" utility for that product as compared to the total weighed utility for all products in the competitive set. The weighting is done using an exponential function. This analysis option is an alternative to the share-of-utility model for frequently purchased products.

The market-share predictions made by both the share-of-utility and logit choice rules are sensitive to the scale range on which utility is measured. The market share prediction of the share-of-utility rule will change if you add a constant value to the computed utility of each product, but it is not altered if you multiply all utility values by a constant. On the other hand, market-share predictions of the logit choice rule are not altered if you add a constant to the utilities, but they are altered if you multiply all utilities by a constant.

In computing market shares, we follow Green and Krieger (1985) who first normalized the utility scale for each respondent such that the least preferred option of each attribute has a utility equal to 0, and the utility scale has a range from 0 to K, where K is the number of attributes.

It is best not to interpret the market-share prediction for a new product in an absolute sense. Instead, view the share in a relative sense—those new products that have higher predicted market shares are likely to perform better in the market than those that have lower predicted shares.

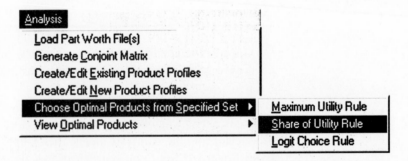

6. After you choose an analysis option, you will see a pie graph showing the market share for the first new-product concept. The following screen shows that the market share for the new-product concept called "Profesnl_1" is 16.44 percent when it is introduced into the market with four existing competitors. Click **Next** to see the graph for the next concept.

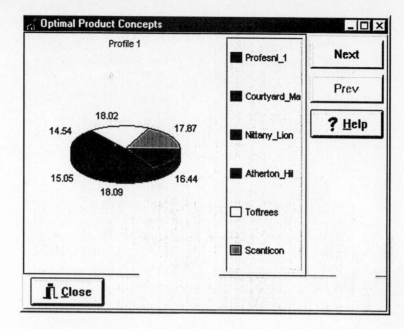

7. You can also do a complete search of all possible product profiles by going to the **Analysis** menu and choosing **View Optimal Products**. If you choose this command the program will select the top four performing product profiles according to the choice rule that you specify.

NOTE: *Products that you have defined in the existing product profiles are excluded from this evaluation.*

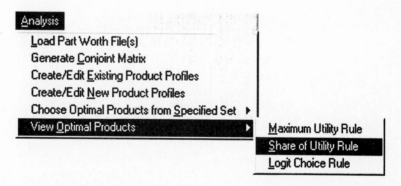

Limitations of the educational version of the software:

Maximum number of attributes:	6
Maximum number of levels per attribute:	4
Maximum number of existing product profiles:	8
Maximum number of new product concepts that can be evaluated:	5,000

References

Green, Paul E. and Wind, Yoram 1975, "New Way to Measure Consumers' Judgments," *Harvard Business Review*, Vol. 53, No. 4 (July-August), pp. 107-117.

Lilien, Gary L. and Rangaswamy, Arvind 1998, *Marketing Engineering: Computer-Assisted Marketing Analysis and Planning*, Chapter 7, Addison Wesley Longman, Reading, Massachusetts.

Wind, Jerry; Green, Paul E.; Shifflet, Douglas; and Scarbrough, Marsha 1989, "The Courtyard by Marriott: Designing a Hotel Facility with Consumer-based Marketing Models," *Interfaces*, Vol. 19, No. 1 (January-February), pp. 25-47.

FORTE HOTEL DESIGN CASE[*]

Forte Executive Innes

Forte Hotels, a large European hotel chain, is developing a new hotel chain in the United States. The chain, named Forte Executive Innes, will combine the ambiance of a European hotel with American functionality and convenience. Forte decided to invest in this hotel chain partly to take advantage of the increasing numbers of business people traveling from Europe to the United States.

Company background

Forte Hotels is the United Kingdom's largest hotel chain. Its hotel brands include Le Meridien, Forte Crest, Forte Posthouse, Forte Agip, and Forte Travelodge. In addition Forte Hotels includes an international group of 80 upscale hotels such as the Watergate Hotel, Washington, D.C., Hyde Park Hotel, London, and King Edward Hotel, Toronto. Recently the company's chairman, Sir Rocco Forte, announced that he plans to sell the Travelodge chain in the United States. In its place Forte Hotels will develop a new chain targeted toward European and American business travelers, Forte Executive Inne.

Forte's strategy in developing the new chain is twofold. European business travelers in the United States will recognize the Forte name and associate it with comfort and service. Forte executives also expect that American business travelers will associate the new chain with "pampering" that is often lacking in the mid-priced hotel chains, while at the same time perceiving the hotel to have all the functionality of American hotel chains. Although the hotels will have a European ambiance, the facilities and services will be comparable to those available in such hotel chains as Hilton, Sheraton, and Courtyard by Marriott.

Preliminary evaluation

A recent survey indicated that the top three reasons business travelers choose a hotel are price, location, and brand name. Forte Executive Innes would be mid-priced, around $100 per night. The company is in the process of securing several prime locations near suburban commercial centers throughout the United States. In addition, the company will leverage the Forte brand name in naming the new chain. Forte now faces the challenge of fine-tuning the specific characteristics

---

[*] This case describes a hypothetical situation. It was developed by Bruce Semisch under the guidance of Professor Arvind Rangaswamy.

of the hotel to insure that it will appeal to both American and European business travelers.

A search of business databases provided some preliminary insights on the preferences of business travelers. Among men (60 percent of business travelers in the United States), price, location, and convenience are among the top reasons why a business traveler might try a new hotel. Women travelers place more emphasis on safety and cleanliness than do men. Although these considerations, combined with the overall image of the brand name, are important in generating trial, it is the hotel's unique characteristics (attributes) that encourage repeat visits. Other recent surveys have suggested a range of potential amenities that interest at least 30 percent of business travelers. These include in-room computer facilities; on-site conference facilities; rooms with well-lit work areas with large desks and swivel chairs; and telecommunication facilities, such as speaker phones and data-ports. A survey by a leading credit card company suggests that about half the European business travelers to the United States look for hotels that will look after them and let them relax. The others tended to look for hotels that would let them finish their business assignments quickly and efficiently. Given these preliminary insights, Forte realized that it needed to thoroughly understand the preferences of the hotel's target market to create a successful new hotel chain.

Conjoint Analysis (Matching hotel attributes to customer preferences)

As a first step, the company decided to explore consumer preferences for five key attributes on which Forte Executive Innes could be differentiated: room type, business amenities, leisure facilities, conveniences and extras, and restaurants and dining. Within each attribute, it defined several different options (Exhibit 1). It did not include hotel features that are common to all existing and proposed hotels among the options. Thus for comparison purposes, it considered hotel room types of roughly the same square-foot area, with data-ports and other facilities in the rooms and front-desk faxing services.

Forte's challenge was to decide which combination of the attribute options in Exhibit 1 would most appeal to its target audience. The management team has authorized you to use conjoint analysis to determine this in a "scientific manner." It has recruited 300 business travelers to participate in the conjoint analysis study. For this exercise, you will use the information obtained from 40 of the respondents (Exhibit 2).

EXERCISES

1. ***Design***: On the **Scenario** menu of the Conjoint Analysis program, choose **Edit Attributes and Levels** to explore the design of this

conjoint study (section 1 of the tutorial). Briefly summarize the advantages and limitations of describing products as bundles of attribute options.

2. ***Utility assessment***: Use the **Utility Assessment** command to explore your own trade-offs for the various attributes and options Forte Inne is considering (section 2 of the tutorial). First complete the prepare task (self-explicated ratings), and then complete the ratings task. Each member of a project group should do a separate utility assessment. When you are finished, note down the final set of weights for each attribute and attribute option.

   Based on your experiences in completing these tasks, summarize the advantages and limitations of conjoint analysis for obtaining preference data from customers.

3. ***Analysis***: Use the **Analysis** menu (section 3 of the tutorial) to assess the viability of the four specific hotel concepts (Profesnl_1, Profesnl_2, Tourist, and Deluxe) that Forte is exploring for the State College area. Base this evaluation on the preferences of a sample of 40 business travelers given in the case and the rough cost estimates summarized in Exhibit 3. The preference data is already included in the hotel.cnj file. The base cost to build each hotel room (without the attributes and options listed in Exhibit 3) is expected to be about $40,000 for a 150 to 200-room hotel, regardless of the mix of room types.

   Identify the optimal product concept from among those Forte is considering. Explain how you arrived at your recommendation.

4. Would you recommend product concepts other than the four Forte is considering for the State College market? Explain how you arrived at your recommendation(s).

5. Summarize the major advantages and limitations of a conjoint study for new-product design. What conditions favor the use of this approach in the hotel industry? (Consider such factors as types of customers and market conditions in responding to this question).

6. After hearing about the study, a manager at Forte claimed that "A conjoint study is a major deterrent to excellence in hotel design. It's a crutch for managers with no vision and conviction. On the surface, it sounds sensible enough: Find out exactly what features customers prefer before you finalize the design. But in practice, this is impossible. Customers cannot tell you what they really prefer without experiencing all the choices available to them. Even if you show them pictures or prototypes, the preferences they express are apt to veer off in the direction of mediocrity. This type of study gives you a Hyundai with a Mercedes grille, Prince tennis rackets endorsed by Ed McMahon, Big Macs with everything, and hotels with no per-

sonality! You would not produce a Mazda Miata, a Hermes tie, or the movie "Jurassic Park" with this technique." Do you agree with this statement? Why or why not?

Reference

Green, Paul E. and Krieger, Abba M. 1986, "Choice Rules and Sensitivity Analysis in Conjoint Simulators," Working Paper, The Wharton School, University of Pennsylvania, Philadelphia, Pennsylvania.

Attribute [Abbreviation]	Possible Options [Abbreviation]

Room type (All same size) [Room]	• Small suite [sm_suite]
	   A small suite with a small bedroom area and a separate sitting area with a couch, TV, and coffee table.
	• Large standard room [lg_room]
	   A room about three feet longer than a standard room with two queen-sized beds.
	• Room with large desk and swivel chair [rm_office]
	   A room of the same dimensions as the large standard room with only one queen-sized bed and a well-lit work area with a large desk and swivel chair in place of the other bed.

Business Amenities [Bus_amen]	• World Wide Web (WWW) access [www_access]
	   A computer complete with software (e.g. Netscape) with access to Internet and the WWW, at a low hourly connection rate ($2 to $3 per hour).
	• Speakerphone in room [sp_phone]
	   A speakerphone for group business discussions.
	• In-room fax machine [room_fax]
	   A fax machine and a private fax number that expires at checkout.

Leisure Facilities [Leisure]	• Exercise room [exerc_room]:
	   A room equipped with Nautilus machines, free weights, stationary bikes, tread mills, stair climbing machines, and a sauna, that is open 24 hours a day.
	• Pool [pool]:
	   A standard rectangular indoor lap pool with shallow and deep ends.
	• Small exercise room and small pool [exerc+pool]:
	   An exercise room that lacks some of the features described above (e.g. no sauna, and fewer machines) and a round pool for recreational swimming, not a lap pool.

Conveniences & Extras [Extras]	• Complimentary shoe shine [shoe_shine]
	   Shoes left at the front desk or outside the room at night are shined and returned by a specified time in the morning.
	• Videotape library [tape_lib]
	   A large selection of tapes will be listed in a catalog in the room and available through room service.
	• Complimentary fruit and cheese bowl. [ft+cheese]
	   A complimentary fruit and gourmet cheese bowl in the room.
	• Free newspaper. [newspaper]
	   A complimentary copy of *USA Today* outside the door.

Restaurant Delivery [Restrn_del]	• Yes [yes]
	   From a book of menus from nearby restaurants, patrons can order food through room service, and a hotel employee will pick up and deliver the food.
	• No [no]
	   No restaurant delivery service available.

EXHIBIT 1
Attributes and Options

	Room	Bus. Amen.	Lei- sure	Ex- tras	Restrn Delivery	Sm Suite	Lg Room	Rm Office	WWW Access	Sp phone	Room Fax	Exer- cise Room	Pool	Exer. + Pool	Shoe Shine	Tape Lib.	Ft+ Che- ese	News- paper	Del. Yes	Del. No
1	47	21	16	11	5	47	0	20	21	0	10	12	16	0	10	0	8	11	5	0
2	23	29	7	18	23	23	0	7	0	15	29	7	0	5	9	5	18	0	0	23
3	15	38	9	21	17	15	0	12	0	14	38	4	0	9	5	7	0	21	0	17
4	20	27	10	20	23	20	0	16	10	0	27	8	10	0	0	12	20	16	23	0
5	21	26	21	21	11	21	10	0	12	26	0	0	21	3	21	9	13	0	0	11
6	22	25	12	22	19	8	0	22	13	25	0	0	12	6	22	11	0	15	0	19
7	33	16	13	33	5	16	0	33	0	16	10	13	0	10	0	11	33	18	0	5
8	24	23	14	24	15	13	0	24	10	23	0	14	0	4	8	0	24	12	15	0
9	34	22	6	22	16	0	12	34	9	22	0	0	5	6	15	0	22	8	16	0
10	26	21	16	19	18	26	0	10	21	0	14	9	16	0	0	14	7	19	18	0
11	11	52	10	17	10	0	9	11	52	13	0	0	8	10	17	6	13	0	0	10
12	19	22	18	24	17	0	14	19	9	0	22	10	18	0	24	5	0	7	17	0
13	28	37	19	12	4	12	0	28	5	0	37	0	19	11	8	12	0	6	4	0
14	30	19	20	13	18	14	0	30	7	0	19	20	10	0	4	6	0	13	0	18
15	47	25	9	12	7	0	7	47	0	25	9	6	0	4	12	8	0	0	0	7
16	34	23	12	14	17	34	0	11	23	13	0	4	12	0	5	0	8	14	17	0
17	27	42	7	8	16	27	0	23	0	13	42	0	4	7	8	6	0	3	0	16
18	34	16	16	21	13	34	0	30	0	16	11	0	16	11	21	0	14	8	13	0
19	50	19	11	8	12	50	27	0	0	19	4	11	0	7	0	8	5	4	12	0
20	34	27	14	10	15	34	0	16	6	27	0	8	0	14	4	0	10	8	0	15
21	33	29	3	26	9	28	0	33	11	29	0	0	1	3	6	0	26	4	0	9
22	22	22	12	24	20	0	16	22	5	0	22	12	6	0	24	8	0	12	0	20
23	31	10	10	18	31	8	0	31	8	0	10	10	4	0	0	7	15	18	31	0
24	20	21	9	41	9	20	0	14	0	7	21	9	0	5	41	13	10	0	0	9
25	31	14	25	18	12	14	31	0	14	0	13	7	25	0	13	0	18	8	12	0
26	29	11	31	16	13	10	0	29	7	11	0	0	31	17	2	9	16	0	13	0
27	18	27	27	14	14	0	7	18	0	27	18	12	0	27	4	9	0	14	0	14
28	27	4	56	10	3	0	27	7	4	0	2	56	19	0	4	10	0	6	3	0
29	16	29	29	12	14	0	16	8	16	29	0	0	29	20	0	12	6	9	14	0
30	45	2	32	2	19	45	0	17	0	2	0	0	15	32	2	0	0	1	0	19
31	16	16	33	13	22	6	16	0	0	16	9	7	0	33	5	0	9	13	0	22
32	19	22	32	11	16	0	19	5	10	22	0	32	16	0	9	11	0	3	16	0
33	43	12	25	8	12	13	43	0	11	0	12	10	25	0	0	8	6	4	0	12
34	37	9	39	3	12	10	37	0	0	9	3	0	39	21	3	0	3	0	12	0
35	17	24	32	15	12	17	7	0	7	24	0	5	0	32	2	15	8	0	0	12
36	72	7	10	5	6	72	43	0	7	6	0	7	0	10	0	0	5	5	0	6
37	36	18	24	8	14	36	18	0	18	8	0	0	11	24	0	6	8	8	14	0
38	25	13	38	12	12	25	0	17	13	0	8	0	20	38	0	10	4	12	0	12
39	20	19	32	18	11	11	20	0	9	0	19	14	0	32	4	0	18	12	11	0
40	32	15	31	12	10	17	32	0	0	15	15	31	0	28	12	7	0	5	10	0

EXHIBIT 2
Preference Data for 40 respondents

	Incremental fixed costs per room ($) at the time of construction	Average expected incremental contribution per day per room ($)
WWW access	2,500	3.00
Speaker phone in room	200	2.00
In-room fax machine	600	2.50
Exercise room	1,500	-2.00
Pool	3,000	-4.00
Small exercise room & small pool	3,500	-4.50
Complimentary shoe shine	30	-0.50
Videotape library	300	-0.50
Complimentary fruit & cheese bowl	100	-5.00
Newspaper	-	-1.00
Restaurant delivery	100	-3.00
No restaurant delivery	-	-

EXHIBIT 3
Cost Data

Chapter 5

TUTORIAL FOR DECISION TREE ANALYSIS

Concept

Decision Tree Analysis is useful to managers choosing among various courses of action when the choice (or sequence of choices) will ultimately lead to some uncertain consequences. The TreeÅge software allows you to take into account the potential *payoffs*, *risks*, and *ambiguities* associated with decisions when the decision process can be broken down into a sequence of actions and events. *Payoffs* are the monetary or other consequences of a decision; *risks* are the potential adverse consequences that may result from the decision because the decision maker lacks control over the consequences of the decision (i.e., he or she doesn't know the outcomes with certainty), and *ambiguities* are imprecise information about payoffs and the degree of risk.

A decision tree analysis typically consists of four steps: (1) structuring the problem as a tree in which the end nodes of the branches are the payoffs associated with a particular path (scenario) along the tree, (2) assigning subjective probabilities to events represented on the tree, (3) assigning payoffs for consequences (dollar or utility value associated with a particular scenario), and (4) selecting course(s) of action based on analyses (e.g., rolling back of the tree, sensitivity analyses, Monte Carlo simulations). We describe each step using the QRS Company in the following example.

Example:

This example is based on Keeney (undated notes). The QRS Company must decide whether or not to introduce a new product now. If it chooses to introduce it, sales will either be high or low. For simplicity, we assume that the firm's objective is to maximize expected profits. The firm is considering a market survey to collect information on expected sales. The market research firm contacted will report one of three results: great, good, or poor, where great means that high sales are likely. Marketing management feels that, if the firm introduces the product now, its probability of high sales is 0.4. The company has had past experience with this market research firm and knows that 60 percent of high-sales products in the past had great survey results, 30 percent had good survey results, and 10 percent had poor survey results. Similarly, 10 percent of its low-sales products had great survey results, 30 percent had good survey results, and 60 percent had poor survey results. If sales are high, the firm expects net profits (excluding the cost of the survey) to be $100,000; if sales are low, it expects a net loss of $50,000 (excluding survey costs).

This problem can be structured as a decision tree in the following exhibit. The chronology of events begins on the left and flows to the right. The first thing that happens is that marketing management must decide whether or not to run a market survey. If it does run a survey, it then learns the results and decides whether or not to introduce the product. Finally, it learns sales results.

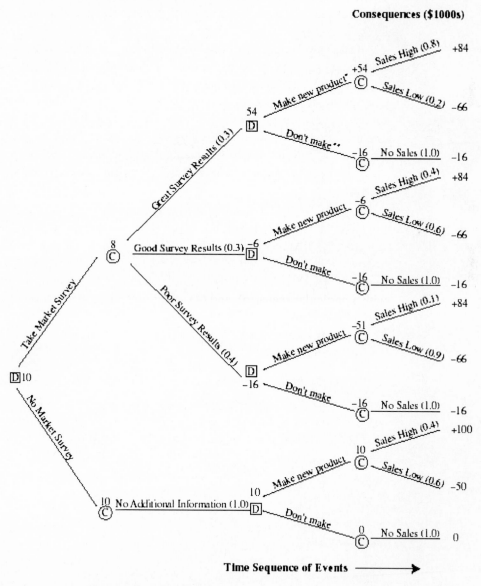

Consequences ($1000s)

** Read as: Introduce new product now.

** Don't introduce new product now; delay introduction or 'kill' the project.

EXHIBIT 1

Structure of decision tree for QRS Company, where the nodes marked D are decision nodes and those marked C are chance nodes.

A decision tree has two types of nodes: decision nodes (marked D), meaning management has control over the course of action, and chance nodes (marked C), where the decision maker has no control.

At the end of each path of the decision tree, the consequences of the several courses of action are indicated. For instance, if the firm runs a market survey and that survey reports great results and the firm manufactures the product and sales are high, the result is a net gain of $84,000: $100,000 less the $16,000 survey cost. All consequences are measured against the do-nothing strategy of no survey, no manufacturing, and no sales.

Beside those segments of the tree beginning at chance nodes are the conditional probabilities (the numbers in parentheses) that the event associated with that segment occurs, given that everything else up to that point in the tree *does* occur. Thus, for instance, the probability that the survey is *great*, given that the firm runs the survey, is 0.3, or 30 percent. The conditional probability that sales are high, given that survey results are great and the firm decides to manufacture, is 0.8, or 80 percent.

To summarize the given information, the firm knows from past experience

$$
\begin{aligned}
p(\text{great survey} \mid \text{high sales}) &= 0.6 \\
p(\text{good survey} \mid \text{high sales}) &= 0.3 \\
p(\text{poor survey} \mid \text{high sales}) &= 0.1 \\
p(\text{great survey} \mid \text{low sales}) &= 0.1 \\
p(\text{good survey} \mid \text{low sales}) &= 0.3 \\
p(\text{poor survey} \mid \text{low sales}) &= 0.6 \\
p(\text{high sales}) &= 0.4 \\
p(\text{low sales}) &= 0.6.
\end{aligned}
$$

To get the probability that the survey would be great, we use the theorem of total probabilities:

$$
\begin{aligned}
p(\text{great survey}) =\ & p(\text{great survey} \mid \text{high sales})p(\text{high sales}) \\
+\ & p(\text{great survey} \mid \text{low sales})p(\text{low sales}) \\
=\ & 0.6 \times 0.4 + 0.1 \times 0.6 = 0.3.
\end{aligned}
$$

Similarly,
$$
\begin{aligned}
p(\text{good survey}) &= 0.3 \\
p(\text{poor survey}) &= 0.4.
\end{aligned}
$$

To get p (great survey | high sales), we use Bayes's theorem:

$$
p(\text{high sales} \mid \text{great survey}) = \frac{p(\text{great survey} \mid \text{high sales})p(\text{high sales})}{p(\text{great survey})}
$$

$$
= \frac{0.6 \times 0.4}{0.3} = 0.8
$$

Similarly, we get

$$p(\text{high sales} \mid \text{good survey}) = 0.4$$
$$p(\text{high sales} \mid \text{poor survey}) = 0.1$$
$$p(\text{low sales} \mid \text{great survey}) = 0.2$$
$$p(\text{low sales} \mid \text{good survey}) = 0.6$$
$$p(\text{low sales} \mid \text{poor survey}) = 0.9.$$

We can now use these probabilities to average out and fold back. The numbers beside each node represent the expected profit associated with being at that node. If we conduct a market survey, have great results, and introduce the product now, then there is an 80 percent chance of high sales, implying a net profit of $84,000, and a 20 percent chance of low sales, with a net loss of $66,000. Thus the expected profit (averaging out) of being at that chance node is

$$0.8 \ (\$84,000) - 0.2 \ (\$66,000) = \$54,000.$$

At the node immediately below, if we have the same great results on the survey and then choose not to manufacture, we will lose $16,000.

Now backing up (folding back) to the decision node before these chance nodes, the firm can either introduce the product with expected profit of $54,000 or not introduce the product now with an expected loss of $16,000. The best choice is to make the product; therefore the expected profit of that decision node is $54,000. In addition, if we fold back to the start, we find the best choice is not to do the survey.

Software

TreeÅge is a comprehensive software package that includes a detailed online help file and an electronic manual. Here we describe only the features that you will need for the ICI case.

NOTE*: To view or print a copy of the complete manual, you will need the original CD on which the marketing engineering software was distributed:*

If you do not have Adobe Acrobat™ installed on your system, run ACROREAD.EXE on the Marketing Engineering CD to install it. Follow the installation instructions that you see on the screen.

*After Acrobat™ is successfully installed, start the Acrobat program. From the **File** menu, select **Open** and open the file manual.pdf from the x:\treeage\manuals directory, where x is the letter representing your CD-ROM drive. Under the **File** menu, select **Print to** print any part of the manual.*

Step 1—Structuring the problem as a decision tree

When you start the program, you will see an empty root node from which you can construct a tree. To load a pre-existing tree go to the **File** menu and select **Open**. (Choose the QRS.TRE file in the ../MktgEng/data directory to familiarize yourself with the software. If you load QRS.TRE, you can go directly to **Step 2**.)

On the **Options** menu, select **Add Branch** or **Insert Branch** to add branches to any node on the tree. To delete a branch, click **Delete Branch**.

Another method for adding branches to a node is to double-click on the node. When the cursor is over the node's symbol, it will change to a branch cursor to indicate that double-clicking will add branches.

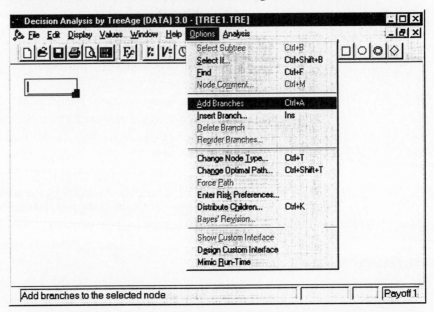

To indicate what a branch stands for, enter descriptive text in the box above it. Place the cursor above the line and click to get the box.

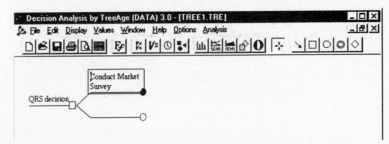

TIP: *Many decision trees have some subtree replication. You can cut and paste a subtree to other locations on the tree. Place the cursor at the root node of the subtree you want to copy and click. Go to the **Options** menu and click **Select Subtree**. Then go to the **Edit** menu and choose **Copy Subtree**. Next place the cursor on the node where you want to insert the subtree and click. Now go to the **Edit** menu and click **Paste**. You*

*can cut and paste subtrees even after you assign names and probabilities to the branches and payoffs to the terminal nodes. (See also the **Clone** command under online **Help**.)*

*The **Edit** menu contains four tree clipboards named Tree clipboard1 to Tree clipboard 4. Thus, you can retain several subtrees at once, each in its own clipboard, to be pasted as needed.*

Step 2—Assigning (conditional) probabilities to branches of the tree

You can insert the probability of an outcome on the branch of the tree in the text box below the line. To get the text box, place the cursor below the line representing a branch and click.

NOTE: *You can enter probabilities only on the branches of a tree that originate from a chance node. A decision tree contains several types of nodes:*

1. *A chance node (shown as a green circle) represents an uncertain or risky event. Branches emanating from a chance node represent all possible (non-overlapping) outcomes of the event.*
2. *A decision node (shown as a blue square) represents a decision the manager faces. Branches emanating from a decision node specify all available (non-overlapping) decision choices.*
3. *A terminal node (shown as a red triangle) represents a final outcome: the end of a path, often referred to as a scenario.*

*To change a node type, click the node, go to the **Options** menu and click **Change Node Type** and select the node type from the available choices. Alternatively, you can click the icon on the toolbar and select the node type you want.*

As an exercise, construct the tree shown below and the one in Exhibit 1:

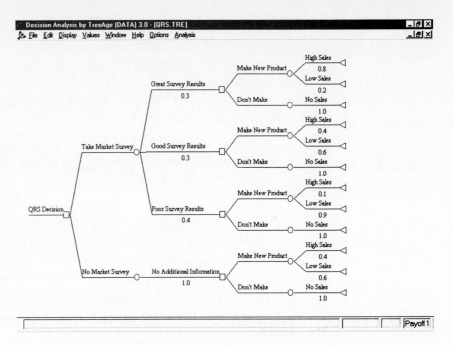

In the rest of the text under **Step 2**, we describe advanced features. You can skip to **Step 3** until you become familiar with the software.

In many cases, you will be uncertain about the accuracy of your probability estimates. Defining the probabilities as variables will enable you to perform sensitivity analyses to help you assess the significance of the uncertainty. To do this, you must define the variable, specify the value(s) it can take, and indicate the location(s) on the decision tree where these values will apply:

1. ***Defining a variable***: Go to the **Values** menu and choose **Define Values**. Click **New** and select **Variable** from the drop-down menu.

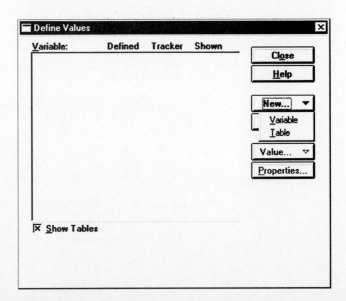

In the **Text Properties** section of the **Properties** dialog box, give your variable a name. If you like, you can also provide a short description or a longer comment, which can be useful for customizing the display,

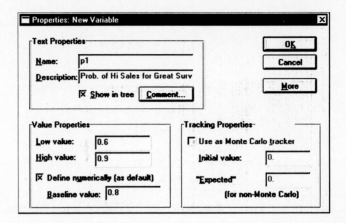

Follow the above procedure to define each variable in your model.

2. ***Specify the default value and, optionally, the range of values a variable takes***. Use the **Value Properties** section to specify a default value (baseline value) for a variable and a range of numeric values to be associated with it. For example, p1 could have the default value of 0.8 and values ranging from 0.6 to 0.9. You can accept or override the suggested range when specifying the parameters of the sensitivity analyses. It is not necessary to provide a range here, although you may find it convenient.

3. ***Indicate the locations on the tree where the values apply***. Click on **Value** and you will be presented with two options. Either you can define a value at a particular node or as a default for the whole tree. If you define a variable at a particular node, the program applies that value of the variable throughout the subtree rooted at the selected node. If you define a variable as the default for the tree, it applies to the entire tree, and its definition resides at the root node. Node-specific definitions are appropriate for probabilities whose values are likely to differ at various points on the tree: for example, the probabilities of high and low sales would depend on whether market research results were favorable. Default definitions are appropriate for probabilities whose values remain constant throughout the tree: for example, the rate of inflation.

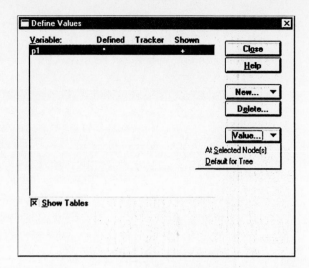

4. ***Associate the variable with probabilities on the tree***:
Insert the variable name in the text box below the branches of
the tree for which the variable will represent the probability
value. In the example below, p1 represents the probability of
"High Sales" under the "Make New Product" and "Great Survey
Results" scenario.

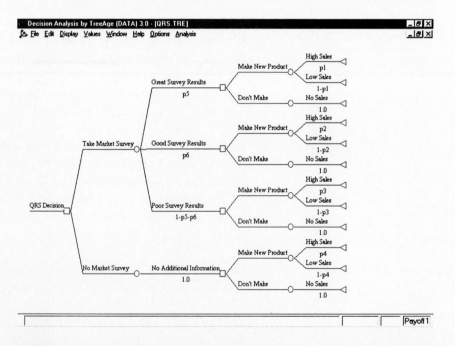

NOTE*: The probabilities along the branches emanating from each
chance node must sum to 1.0. Thus, if two branches emanate from a
chance node, you can assign one the variable p1 and the other (1 - p1).*

It is very important to make the variable assignments at the correct
nodes. For this, you need to understand how the program uses variables
in making calculations.

When the program encounters a variable in a probability field during calculations, it searches for the value assignment beginning with the node immediately to the right of the probability field and moves from there leftward to the root node. For a given variable, the program accepts the first definition (value assignment) that it locates as it makes this traversal. Thus, the program will disregard any definitions closer to the terminal node than the node immediately to the right of the probability field in question.

As a general rule, you should avoid using the same variable to define the probability of more than one event. Thus, if you have two subtrees representing the same uncertainty (high versus low sales) but the probability values are different, you should use different variables.

Step 3—Assigning payoffs (preferences) for scenarios

If you are sure about the dollar value (payoff) associated with a scenario, first select the terminal node (place the cursor on the node and click) and then go to the **Options** menu and select **Change Node Type**. You can also click on the 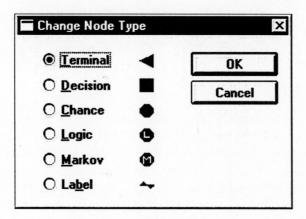 icon to change the node type. You will see the following dialog box:

Select the terminal node option (red triangle) and click **OK**.

You will be prompted to enter a numerical value for **Payoff 1**. You can then enter the sure payoffs (You can associate up to four different payoffs with each scenario (e.g., dollar value, costs, utility value, or payoff realized by a partner firm). In the following example, we selected the terminal node under High Sales under the Great Survey Results scenario, and entered the value 84.

Enter a payoff for each terminal node.

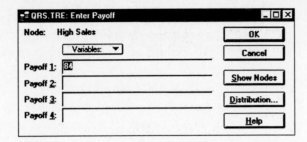

In the rest of the text under **Step 3**, we describe advanced features. You can skip to **Step 4** until you become familiar with the software.

For conducting sensitivity analyses, you can define variables to denote payoffs. The procedure for defining variables for payoffs is the same as the one we described for assigning variables for probabilities. In the following example, we will use the variable v1 to represent payoffs realized under High Sales and with No Market Survey. (You can also use algebraic expressions of defined variables (e.g., *v1 + v2 - v3*) to represent more complex payoffs).

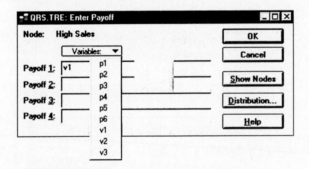

For variables used in calculating payoffs for a scenario, the program will search each node in the scenario, beginning with the terminal node and traversing leftward to the root node, looking for numeric definitions for each relevant variable. For a given variable, the program will accept the first definition (value assignment) that it locates on this traversal. Thus, if the same construct will have different values at two different nodes on the tree, it is best to define two separate variables that apply at those nodes. For example, if unit costs of production are higher at higher volumes, then the cost figures in scenarios with high sales should have larger numbers than cost figures in scenarios that call for lower sales.

Click the **Distribution** button to specify the frequency with which values of the variable would be selected in Monte Carlo analyses. In the example below, we first selected the **Normal** distribution from the palette of distributions and then specified a mean of -66 and a standard deviation of 5.0 for variable v1.

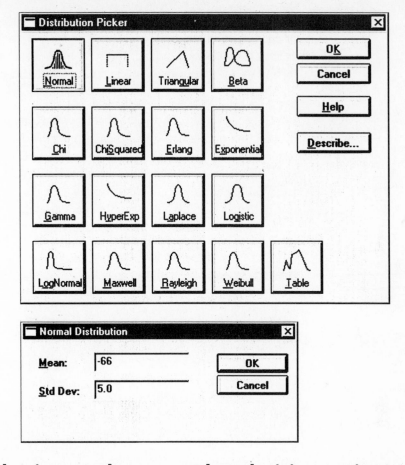

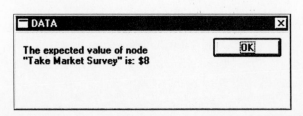

Step 4—Conducting analyses to select decision option(s)

You can conduct many types of analyses with the TreeÅge software. We will describe those you are most likely to use for the ICI exercise. To learn about other types of analyses, play around with the other commands on the **Analysis** menu, which are described in the online help files.

Calculate the expected value of a node: Click on a node, go to the **Analysis** menu, and select **Expected Value**. A dialog box will show the expected value; in this example, the expected value of the Take Market Survey node is $8.

NOTE: *In calculating the expected value, the program uses the baseline values of variables or the mean values of distributions associated with the variables.*

Rolling back the tree: Instead of calculating the expected value of each node in the tree individually, you can calculate and display the expected values and probabilities of all nodes simultaneously. To do this, go to the **Analysis** menu and click **Roll Back**. (Alternatively, you can click on the ![O] icon on the tool bar.)

Once you roll back the tree, you will see three additional pieces of information on the tree: (1) the expected payoffs (in dollars or other appropriate units) shown in a rectangular box at each chance and decision node, (2) the payoff and the overall probability for each terminal node, and (3) the path along the tree that leads to the highest expected payoff (the branches that are not along this path are marked with the symbol \\). In this example, the "optimal" decision is to make the new product without conducting a market survey.

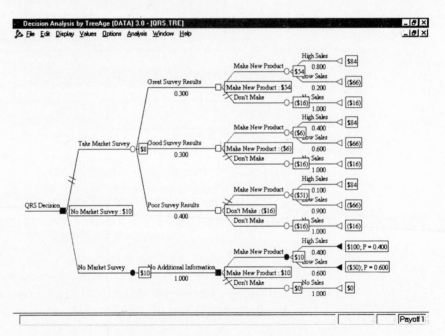

Sensitivity analyses: The TreeÅge software offers several options for conducting sensitivity analyses to determine which factors have great impact on the decisions. The most common way to do this is to select a node and then go to the **Analysis** menu and select **Sensitivity Analysis**. You will then have four choices: (1) analyzing the effects of a change in one variable (One-way); (2) analyzing the effects of changes in any two variables simultaneously (Two-way); (3) analyzing the effects of changes in any three variables simultaneously (Three-way); and (4) Tornado diagram, which is a set of one-way sensitivity analyses on any subgroup of variables in your decision tree. We describe the one-way graphs and Tornado diagrams.

One-Way Sensitivity Analysis: If you choose **One-way**, you will see the following screen.

NOTE: *It is important to first specify the node at which this analysis will apply. Typically you would select the root node to see the impact of the sensitivity analysis on the overall decision.*

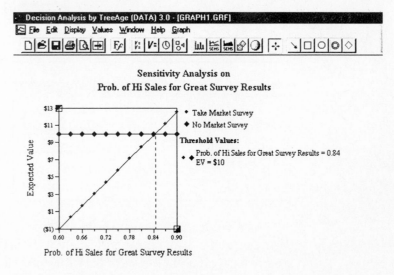

After you specify the variable of interest and its range of variation, click **OK**. You will then see a chart showing how the expected value of each decision option changes as the value of the selected variable changes.

In the following example, the analysis indicates that if p1 (probability of High Sales given Great Survey Results) is equal to a little over 0.84, then it may pay to conduct a test market survey.

On the **File** menu, click **Close** to get back to the decision tree display.

Tornado Diagram: An alternative way to conduct sensitivity analysis is the Tornado diagram, which is a set of mini-sensitivity analyses set forth in a single graph. It can include all or a subset of the variables defined in your tree. You specify which variables are to be included in the analysis and assign a range of values to each of them. In the resulting graph, each variable analyzed is represented by a horizontal bar. Each bar represents the range of possible outcomes generated by varying the related variable. A wide bar indicates that the associated variable has a large potential effect on the expected value of the decision. (This is called a tornado diagram because the bars are arranged in order with the widest bar at the top and narrowest bar at the bottom, resulting in a funnel-like appearance). A vertical dotted line is drawn on the graph to indicate the expected value at the selected node (often the root node).

To construct a tornado diagram, select the chance node or decision node at which you want to construct the diagram. Next from the **Analysis** menu, select **Tornado Diagram**, and then select **Variables to Analyze**. Click each variable to be included (from **Available Variables**) and then click **Add>>**. You will be prompted to specify the range of variation for each variable.

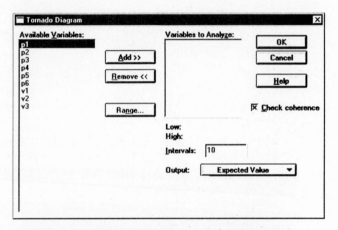

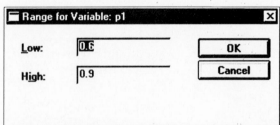

Once you enter the appropriate information, the program will display the results of the sensitivity analysis as bar graphs indicating the expected payoff as the values of the variable(s) change.

NOTE: *The vertical dotted line at the selected node is the "fulcrum" that allows you to view the impact of each variable relative to the original (baseline) expected value. Thus, although the range of p1 is from 0.6 to 0.9, it affects the expected value of the decision only for values from 0.84 to 0.9 - the range in which the expected value of the decision becomes higher than 10, the baseline.*

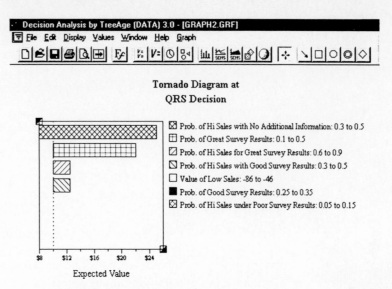

Tornado Diagram at QRS Decision

☒ Prob. of Hi Sales with No Additional Information: 0.3 to 0.5
⊞ Prob. of Great Survey Results: 0.1 to 0.5
▨ Prob. of Hi Sales for Great Survey Results: 0.6 to 0.9
◩ Prob. of Hi Sales with Good Survey Results: 0.3 to 0.5
☐ Value of Low Sales: -86 to -46
■ Prob. of Good Survey Results: 0.25 to 0.35
☒ Prob. of Hi Sales under Poor Survey Results: 0.05 to 0.15

Expected Value

Monte Carlo analysis: In Monte Carlo analysis, the model runs a number of simulated trials. The result of each trial is a single scenario, selected according to the probabilities specified in the model. On most decision trees, no specified outcome corresponds to the expected value. The results from the simulation are a distribution of payoffs, rather than a single expected value. Over many simulation trials, the average result will fall very close to the expected value, but you will also obtain information about the variance around the expected value. You can find more details about the Monte Carlo analysis in the online help and in the detailed manual for the program that you can print out as we described at the beginning of this tutorial.

Limitations of the educational version of the software

The educational (demonstration) version of TreeÅge is identical to the full version in most respects, except:

- You cannot save any documents. Once you complete an exercise, you cannot store the tree for future use (although you can print out a copy from which you can reconstruct the tree). So, do not exit the program until you are sure you have completed all analyses.
- The maximum size tree you can create manually is 50 nodes.
- The maximum size tree you can open is 125 nodes. We have included several example files (with extension *.tre) that you can open to learn more about how decision trees are used in various application areas.

ICI AMERICAS R&D PROJECT SELECTION CASE*

ICI America is a subsidiary of the British-based Imperial Chemical Industries, Ltd (ICI). In 1992, ICI's sales totaled $11.2 billion, making it one of the largest chemical companies in the world. The company reported a net income of $218 million for 1992 before exceptional items and discontinued operations. Its North American subsidiaries included US-based ICI Americas (primarily in polyester film, pharmaceuticals, and specialty chemicals) and Canadian Industries Ltd. (strong in explosives, pulp and paper chemicals, and environmental services). The Canadian subsidiary marketed industrial explosives (e.g., for use in mining operations) throughout North America. ICI Americas focused on the military explosives market. The post-cold-war era has reduced this subsidiary's growth opportunities. To survive within a fast growing company, it needed new products, especially for nonmilitary applications.

ICI Americas' Canadian subsidiary discovered a new but unpatentable application for one of its products (anthraquinine or AQ): used as an agent for reducing pulp mill water pollution. AQ acts by reacting with paper and pulp waste pollutants to form solids that can be filtered out of the paper-mill waste stream.

If Canadian Industries could develop the AQ product and process on a commercial scale, it could create a large global market. Reducing the pollution from pulp and paper processing was a major goal of environmental regulatory authorities worldwide. For example, the state-of-the-art Kraft process produced offensive odors and an effluent that reddened streams. AQ was distilled from coal tar and used principally in manufacturing dyes. Coal tar is a byproduct of coke production, and coke is used exclusively to make steel. Hence ICI's current AQ capacity was directly related to the world demand for steel.

At the time, all the AQ produced in the world would have satisfied only a small portion of the unpatented and unconfirmed market for the product as a pollution reducing agent. One of ICI's competitors, BASF, had an alternative process for synthesizing AQ; if ICI did not move rapidly, BASF might preempt ICI's potential leadership position.

ICI needed to do a quick analysis to decide whether to go ahead with its R&D expenditures or to abandon the project.

The following were the primary issues it considered in making this decision:

- Would market tests confirm that there was a significant market for the product?
- Could the company develop a new process for making this product that was technically feasible?

---

* Adapted from Hess (1993).

- Even if there were a significant market and the process were technically feasible, would the company's board sanction an investment in a new plant necessary to produce the product on a commercial scale?
- Assuming the answers to the above questions were all yes and the plant was built, would the venture turn out to be successful?

Assuming that each of these four issues had a yes or no answer, the management team estimated the probabilities for each event (Exhibit 1).

Event	Probability
Significant market	0.6 ± 0.15
Technically feasible	0.15 ± 0.10
Board sanctions plant expenditures	0.8 ± 0.2
Commercial success	0.8 ± 0.2

EXHIBIT 1
Probabilities for Water Pollution Problem

The following primary economic factors affected the profitability of the venture:

- The research expenses to identify a new production process for the product
- The marketing research cost to determine whether there was a significant market
- The process development costs, including presanction engineering
- The commercial development costs, both before and after the board's sanction
- The venture value (net present value) if successful

Estimates of these values are given in Exhibit 2. The plus-or-minus signs show the degree of uncertainty about the values. (All dollar values are in millions of dollars.)

Expense or Gain	Net Present Value (Million \$)
Research expense	\$ 1.5 ± 0.40
Marketing Research expense	\$ 0.2 ± 0.50
Process development expense (presanction)	\$ 3.0 ± 0.75
Commercial development expense (presanction)	\$ 0.5 ± 0.25
Commercial development expense (postsanction)	\$ 1.0 ± 0.25
Value if successful	\$ 25.0 ± 12.50

EXHIBIT 2
Monetary Estimates for Water Pollution Problem

The decisions and actions the firm considered were to decide whether to abandon the product now or:

- To spend on research and marketing development. If marketing research indicates an insignificant market for the product, then abandon the project.
- If process development research indicates that the project is not technically feasible (given positive marketing research), then abandon the project.
- If the process appears technically feasible, then invest in process development. If that research indicates that the process is technically infeasible, cut expenses and quit.
- If the project is technically feasible, spend on process development and begin commercial development. If the company board then declines to sanction the money for the new plant, cut expenses and quit.
- If the board approves, spend on further commercial development. By this time the company has made all of its decisions. If the venture turns out to be a commercial success then it gains the venture value for a success (less expenses so far). Otherwise the company has lost the money spent so far, but that is all.

EXERCISES

ICI managers thought that a decision tree analysis would be appropriate for the problem they faced. Construct a decision tree to represent this problem structure. The managers are interested in the following questions:

1. What is the maximum ICI should invest in presanction process development?
2. What decision would the model recommend under optimistic, pessimistic, and best-guess scenarios?

3. Which probability and payoff estimates have the most impact on the decision?

4. What should ICI do and why?

Reference

Hess, Sidney W. 1993, "Swinging on the Branch of a Tree: Project Selection Applications," *Interfaces*, Vol. 23, No. 6 (November-December), pp. 5-12.

Chapter 6

TUTORIAL FOR GEODEMOGRAPHIC SITE PLANNING

CONCEPT

In selecting a physical location for an outlet, a firm makes two decisions: it chooses a market area, such as a city, region, or country, in which to establish an outlet, and then it chooses a specific site within that location. Firms can now use formal models in making location decisions because of the availability of computerized geodemographic databases. These databases overlay demographic, and other types of data (e.g., psychographic), on a geocoded database containing the latitude and longitude of most households and firms in the United States. Combining these databases with quantitative computer models, such as the gravity model, enables managers to carefully evaluate alternative retail location options.

The gravity model helps firms to evaluate the combined effects of factors such as customer profiles, store image, drive times, and the location of competing retailers, on the potential value of a site. In its basic form, the model postulates that the probability that customer i (or more generally, customers in geographic zone i) will choose a store j is given by:

$$p_{ij} = \frac{V_{ij}}{\sum_{n \in N} V_{in}} \tag{1}$$

where

p_{ij} = probability (proportion of times) customers in geographic zone i will choose the store at the jth location

V_{ij} = an index to indicate the attractiveness (also called value or utility) of store j to customers in zone i

N = the set of stores that will compete with the proposed new store.

r

Specifically, the value (V_{ij}) depends on several key factors. An important factor will be the size of the store (or shopping center) at location j; the larger the store, the higher the attractiveness. Larger stores typically offer greater variety and better prices. Another important factor is the distance from an individual's home to each of the competing outlets, including a proposed new outlet. The larger this distance, the less attractive a store becomes to individuals in zone i. Finally, the model permits the use of various parameters to modify the relative impact of store size and distance. Thus customers in a geographical area will be "pulled" (whence, the term gravity model) towards a store with higher probability if it is located closer to their homes, it is larger, and its retail image is more attractive relative to existing competitors. A specific form of V_{ij} in equation (1) that is used in practice is given below:

$$p_{ij} = \frac{S_j^\alpha / D_{ij}^\beta}{\sum_{n \in N} S_j^\alpha / D_{in}^\beta} \tag{2}$$

where

p_{ij} = probability that individuals in zone i will choose store at the *jth* location

S_j = size of store at location j; more generally, this can be some index of store image

D_{ij} = distance of store j from the center of zone i (more generally, this may be viewed as ease of access to the store, rather than just distance)

α = a parameter to "tune" the impact of size (or image) on the consumers' decision to patronize stores

β = a parameter to "tune" the impact of distance (or ease of access), on the decision to patronize stores

Although gravity models have been around for many years, the recent development of geodemographic databases only now make it feasible to apply these models broadly. Without these databases it is difficult to specify exact geographic areas for analysis, and it is cumbersome to obtain distance and demographic data for a large number of geographic zones and stores. Managers are no longer constrained to evaluate store attractiveness by traditional geographic units such as census tracts or zip codes. Newer databases offer finer detail such as latitude and longitude corresponding to every geographic entity, and grid cells to produce highly accurate boundaries.

To develop a gravity model, you have to follow several general steps. The software allows you to implement these steps:

Step 1—Define the market area
Identify a suitable geographic area that is likely to be served by the proposed outlet, and divide that area into its constituent zones. Ideally, the zones should be relatively homogeneous in their demographic characteristics and in the availability of competitive stores and movement barriers (e.g., rivers, railway lines, high-crime neighborhoods).

Step 2—Obtain data about existing stores that are potential competitors to proposed store

In particular, get data on the location, size, sales, and other characteristics of each competing store within the market area.

Step 3—Compute distances

Compute distances from each store to each zone. The accompanying software automatically computes distances once the zones and locations of stores are specified.

Step 4—Calibrate the gravity model

Calibrate the gravity model on the existing competitors in the market area. Specifically, choose a set of parameter values for α and β that fit the existing data well. Starting values can be $\alpha = 1$ and $\beta = 1$, unless there is reason to believe that other values are more likely to recover the current market shares of the competitors. For the chosen values of the parameters, compute p_{ij} from equation (2) using the size and distance information gathered in steps 2 and 3.

1. Compute market shares for each of the existing competitors by aggregating p_{ij}'s as follows:

$$m_j = \frac{\sum\limits_{i \in I} p_{ij} T_j}{\sum\limits_{j \in J} \sum\limits_{i \in I} p_{ij} T_j} \tag{3}$$

   T_j is a measure of sales potential in zone j, I is the set of zones in the market area, and J is the number of existing stores in the market area. Any suitable index available in the database may be used for measuring potential (T_j) in each zone. In some cases, it may be a general index such as average annual expenditure per household or total households in a zone. In other cases, it may be a product-specific index. Potential can even be *relative* measures of demographic variables, such as age or income, that are indexed to an average value of 100.

2. Check that the model produces market shares m_j that are consistent with the actual market shares of the existing competitors. If not, change the values of parameters α and β and repeat Step 4 until the procedure settles on a realistic set of values for α and β.

Step 5—Evaluate sales potential of a new store at various locations

Introduce a new store k at a proposed location into the model, and re-compute p_{ij}'s using the estimated α and β. Compute the sales potential for the new store ($= \sum\limits_{i \in I} p_{ik} T_k$). Repeat this process, if required, by considering other locations for the new store.

Step 6—Select the location of the new store

Select the location of the new store where sales potential, $\sum_{i \in I} p_{ik} T_k$, is highest.

Software: SCAN/US

The gravity model in Scan/US uses a Microsoft Excel macro to evaluate the market shares for up to 80 sites in a single run. After you specify the location of the competing retail stores, the model can compute the required distances internally using its databases. However, you must provide an index of each store's attractiveness.

Scan/US is a comprehensive software program for geodemographic analysis. It includes a detailed online help file. Here we describe only the features that you will need for the J&J Family Video exercise.

NOTE*: To view or print a copy of the complete manual, you will need the original CD on which the marketing engineering software was distributed:*

If you do not have Adobe Acrobat™ installed on your system, run ACROREAD.EXE on the Marketing Engineering CD to install it. Follow the installation instructions that you see on the screen.

*After Acrobat™ is successfully installed, start the Acrobat program. From the **File** menu, select **Open** and open the file manual.pdf from the x:\scanus\manuals directory, where x is the letter representing your CD-ROM drive. Under the **File** menu, select **Print** to print any part of the manual.*

In the J&J Family Video exercise, you will build a gravity model to locate a new video store in the Phoenix, Arizona metropolitan area. This tutorial describes the three steps that you should follow to complete the exercise:

1. Setting up the data for the gravity model
2. Using Microsoft Excel to build the gravity model
3. Mapping the results of the gravity model

Insert your Marketing Engineering CD in the CD-ROM drive. From the **Model** menu, select **Geodemographic Site Planning** to see the following screen:

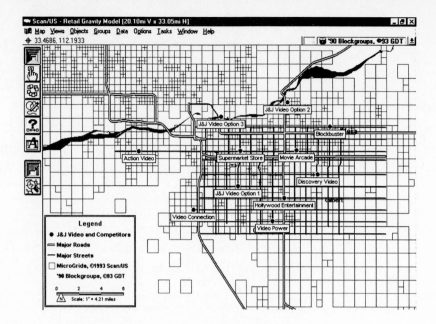

Step 1—Setting up the data for the gravity model

To set up the gravity model, you first create or load the specific geographical area you want to work with. Next, you add various types of data, called layers, to the specified geography. You should then load a file indicating the locations of the retail sites (if it is not already loaded) as the location layer. We have completed these tasks for the J&J Family Video exercise. If this exercise is not automatically loaded when you open the program, go to the **Map** menu and **select J&J Family Video Exercise**.

NOTE: *Gain familiarity with the software before you attempt to set up your own study area and retail site options. Follow the instructions available in the online* **Help** *menu. Briefly, the steps are: 1) Select an area of the US map for study, 2) Select the geographic features you want to include for analysis (e.g., zip centroids, major streets), 3) Indicate the location of various retail sites of interest, and 4) Create and name a new location layer.*

Specify the set of competitive sites to be used in the analysis (*Location Layer*): Make locations the active layer by clicking on the arrow in the upper right corner of the screen and selecting **J&J Video and Competitors**.

Next, select the set of retail sites (video stores) that you want to include in your analysis. To do this, first define a group that contains the selected stores. From the **Groups** menu, choose **New Grouping,** name the grouping, e.g., J&J Sites 1, and click **OK**. Go to the **Groups** menu, click **New Group** and name the group, e.g., All competitors. You can specify many different groups within one grouping.

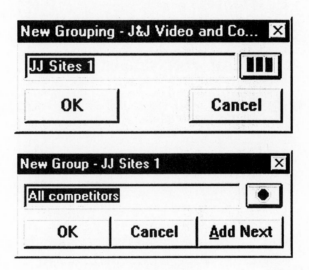

Click **OK**. This should bring you back to the original screen and in group mode (click the group mode icon [icon] on the left side of the screen, if it is not already activated). Now you are ready to specify the sites to be used for the analysis under the group name you provided. It is convenient to first activate the Group-By Polygon submode([icon]) and draw a polygon around the selected video stores by dragging the mouse while pressing the left mouse button. (For the present, select for analysis all the stores that you see on the screen.)

Specify the geographic area you want to include for analysis (Consumer layer): Here you have two options: You can either specify the entire geography already included in the J&J Family Video exercise, or you can select a part of this area.

Option 1: Using the entire geography in the J&J Family Video exercise: (Until you become familiar with the software, we suggest that you select the entire geography for analysis). Here, simply copy the distances from the location layer (J&J Video and competitors) to the consumer layer (MicroGrid layer), which contains information about where people live in the study area. To do so, make locations (i.e., **J&J Video and Competitors**) the active layer at the right upper corner of the screen. Go to the **Objects** menu and select **Copy Distance**. You will see the following box:

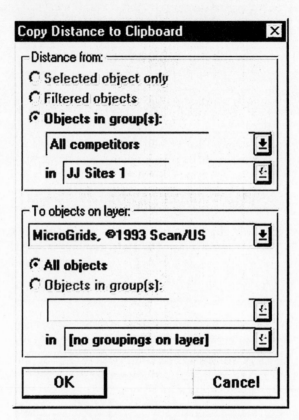

Copy the distance information from **Objects in groups** (e.g., J&J Sites) to **All objects** on the consumer layer (MicroGrid layer), by choosing **MicroGrids, ©1993 Scan/US** from the drop down menu.

Click **OK** to proceed.

Option 2: Using a subset of the geography in the J&J Family Video exercise: Instead of computing distances for all geographical units in the consumer layer, you can also first create a group on the consumer layer and load the distance information from the location layer to the newly defined group on the consumer layer. To do this, click the arrow in the upper right corner of the screen and select the MicroGrid layer:

Go to the **Groups** menu and select **New Grouping** and give the MicroGrid grouping a name:

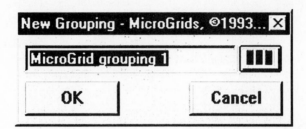

Click the **Group-By Polygon** button (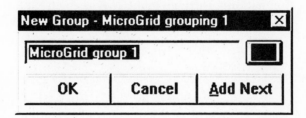) and draw a polygon around the selected geography by dragging the mouse while pressing the left mouse button. Once you have defined a closed polygon, the system will ask you to give a name to the group, for example, MicroGrid group 1:

Click **OK**, and you will see a screen highlighting in red the area you selected:

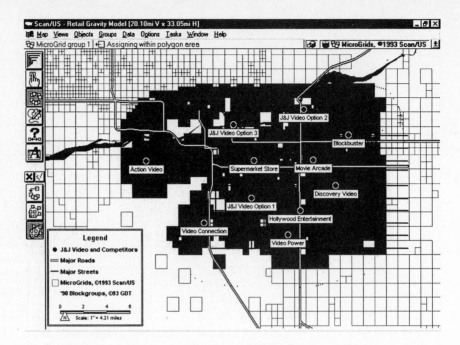

To run the gravity model, you have to copy data containing distances from stores to the MicroGrids to the consumer layer (e.g., a selected group in the MicroGrids layer). This data is then made available to the Excel routine that runs the gravity model. You need to make sure that the location layer, i.e., J&J Video and Competitors, is activated by clicking the arrow in the right upper corner and choosing **J&J Video and Competitors**. Next, go to the **Objects** menu and choose **Copy Distance**. You will see the following box:

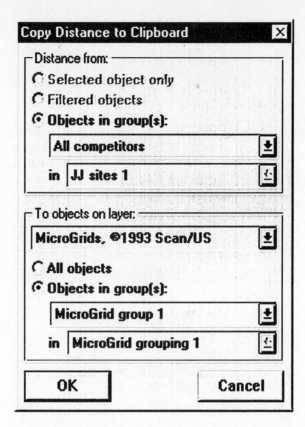

Select **Objects in group(s)** and specify the group and the grouping in the MicroGrid layer you want to include in the analysis. If you select a small geographical area as a group, the gravity model will calculate estimates only for that specific group (area), thus reducing its computation time. Click **OK**.

Step 2—Using Excel to build the gravity model

You build the gravity model using a Microsoft Excel macro. First, you must enter data on store attractiveness indices for each site and the attractiveness and distance impact coefficients.

The distance impact coefficient indicates how much ease of access to a store (site) would influence a consumer's decision to buy from that store. The higher this coefficient, the faster the decline in consumer's utility for a site as its distance from the consumer's home base increases. For example, in a rural area, people commonly travel five miles or more to a store; in a metropolitan area, they do not. The distance impact coefficient in a rural area might be 1.5, while in a metropolitan area it might be 2.0 or higher.

The Scan/US Gravity Model Assistant, a Microsoft Excel macro, generates a data file containing the gravity model estimates, which can then be displayed within the Scan/US program.

On **Tasks** menu, choose **Build Gravity Model.** Microsoft Excel will launch and bring up the Scan/US Gravity Model Assistant.

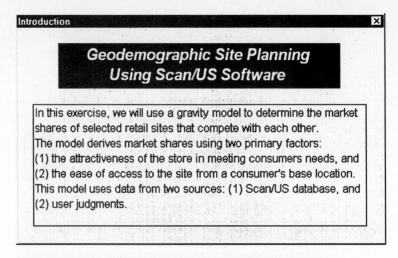

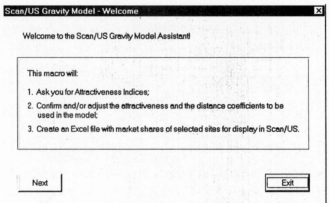

Click **Next**. If you now see a screen listing several fields for Attractiveness Index Data, select the Store ID field. Click **Next**.

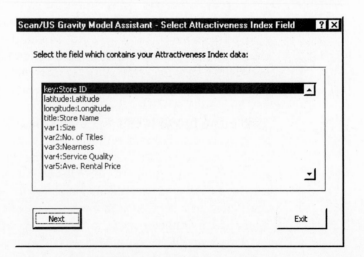

Fill in the attractiveness index for each store on a suitable scale (1-100 is typical, with higher numbers indicating more attractive stores) based on your best judgment about the attractiveness of each store.

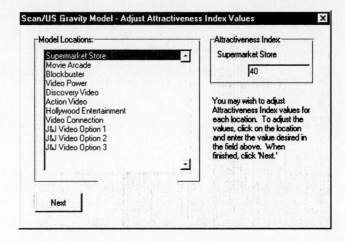

Click **Next** to get to this screen:

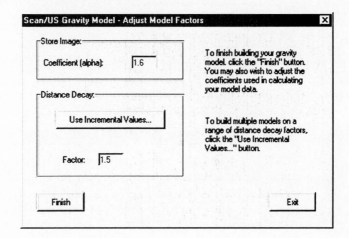

Enter your best guesses as to how store attractiveness (image) and distance influence store choice, choosing alpha and beta coefficients to reflect these influences. You can choose a single value for the beta coefficient, or choose multiple values in a selected range to represent varying degrees of influence of distance on store choice. For the latter case, click **Use Incremental Values** and specify the range:

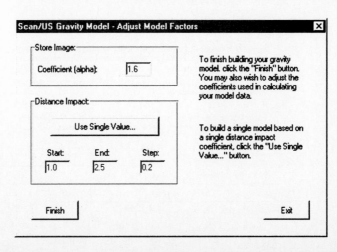

(If you choose a range of values for distance impact, save each set of results under a different Excel 4.0 file at the end of the model run).

Click **Finish** to continue.

The model now starts its computations using the distances generated by Scan/US and the attractiveness indices and the alpha and beta coefficients that you provided. Processing may take several minutes (or even hours) depending on the number of geographic entities included in the analysis. For the J&J Family Video exercise, it should take only a few minutes. The status bar at the bottom of the screen indicates the progress.

When data processing is completed, the Gravity Model Assistant prompts you to save your gravity model table. Change the path in the **Save in** box to the \MktgEng\Scanus\Userdata folder and be sure to set the **Save as Type** to Microsoft Excel 4.0 Worksheet. Enter a filename and click **Save**.

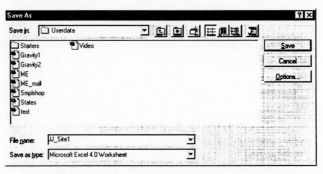

At this point, you are given the option to restart the Excel macro to obtain model results under a different set of attractiveness indices and alpha and beta parameters. To restart the excel macro, click **Back to the Beginning**. Save each run under separate Excel 4.0 worksheets. For the J&J Family Video exercise, you have to run the model at least four times, once with just the existing stores (i.e., by setting the attractiveness indices to zero for the three new sites being considered by Jack and Jeri) and once for each store location option available for J&J Family Video (i.e., by setting the attractiveness indices to zero for the two new sites not included in an analysis).

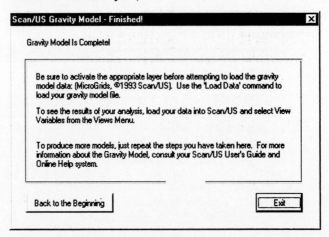

Click **Exit** to get back to Scan/US.

Step 3—Mapping the results of the gravity model

To view the model's market share estimates in Scan/US, you need to load the gravity model results (which are in the saved Microsoft Excel file) to the consumer layer (MicroGrids) and create a new thematic view.

1. Click the arrow in the upper right corner of the screen and choose MicroGrids (the consumer layer) from the drop down menu.

2. Go to the **Data** menu and choose **Load Data**. Switch to the …\MktgEng\Scanus\Userdata folder and select one of the gravity model files you saved in Excel. (To change directories, check the **Directories** option first). Click **OK**.

3. Go to the **Views** menu and click **New Thematic**.

NOTE: *If you grouped objects in the consumer layer when you set up the model, be sure to select **Analyze: Grouped objects in grouping** to view the selected area.*

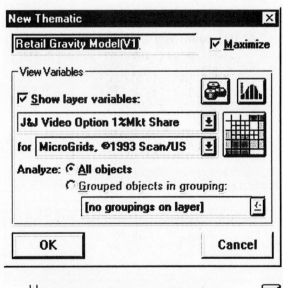

To see how each geographical area contributes market share to a specific site location, you can stratify geographical areas using a color scheme. First select the variable whose geographic distribution you want to view—either estimated market shares for all stores, or for selected stores. In the example above, we have selected **Estimated % Market Shares** for Video Store Option 1. Next, click the **Strata Manager** button ▦.

You can change the range of values that are assigned to a particular color by dragging the appropriate black dumbbell up or down with the mouse. After you finish specifying the parameters, click **OK**.

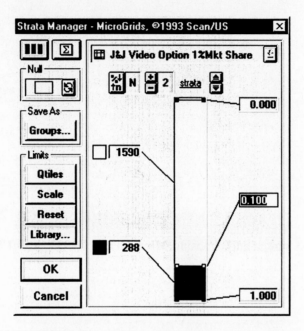

Click **Groups** and assign a name to the group.

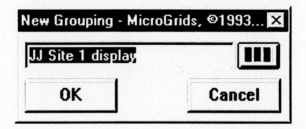

Click **OK**. You will now see the selected geography highlighted with the color scheme you specified showing how market shares for J&J video store option 1 varies by geographical units.

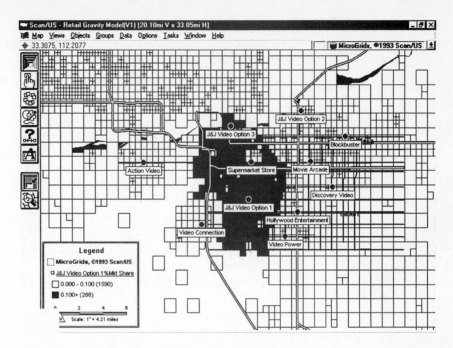

Viewing a group's data: You can also use Scan/US to automatically aggregate the data for each object in a group to create a group summary. First, ensure that the data are attached to the active layer. For example, if you want to investigate the results of the gravity model, activate the MicroGrids layer by clicking on the arrow at the upper right corner of the screen and choosing **MicroGrids, ©1993 Scan/US** from the drop down menu.

The market share estimates for each group are loaded into this layer.

Next click the group mode button: ![button]. Select an existing grouping or create a new group for which you wish to see summary information. For example, if you want to look at market share estimates for a certain area extending over many MicroGrids, you should build a group containing the MicroGrids that lie in the area of interest. Next, go to the **Views** menu and click **QuickLook** to see the active group's data.

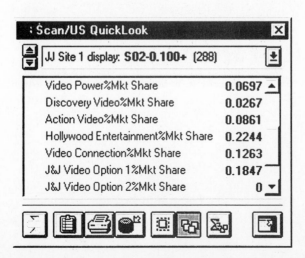

(**Estimated %Market Shares** gives the value for the primary contours, i.e., it is the highest market share estimate reached by any of the competitors in the set.)

You can switch between viewing the data for the active group or of an object (e.g., a selected MicroGrid) by clicking on the "Show Group" button (⊞) or "Show Object" button (left).

Advanced analyses: Customizing your data in Excel

You can get further insights about the sales potential of a site if you index the estimated choice probabilities from the gravity model with demographic information available from the Scan/US database. For instance, for the J&J Video exercise, you can index your probability estimates by taking into account the density of family households with children. You can also calculate potential sales using the probability values and data from the Scan/US retail potential database. To conduct these analyses, use Microsoft Excel to create your own customized data set or to merge your data with the data provided by Scan/US.

NOTE: *There are various databases commercially available that offer information—beyond that contained in the Scan/US BasePak—that can aid your analyses, e.g., data about household expenditures by product category. Some of these databases (e.g., Scan/US retail potential database), come with this educational version of Scan/US but are restricted to the Washington DC and Phoenix, AZ areas.*

In the following section, we explain how to combine data from a Scan/US application with your own data. Principally, you need to know:

1. How to group a subset of the Scan/US product databases and export it to Excel for further manipulation

2. How to prepare your own Excel data for import into the Scan/US program

3. How to display your data by creating a thematic view (see previous sections)

Specifying data for export to Excel

First, you need to indicate which data to include in the analysis. The following example considers only the MicroGrids that have probability values of more than 10 percent for patronizing J&J Video Option 1. You can limit the amount of data to use in an analysis by "hiding strata." (Alternatively, you can select a geographical area by grouping objects (e.g., MicroGrids) as we described earlier.)

"Hiding strata" is a useful way of focusing an analysis on a specific set of objects. You can hide strata only when a variable's strata, instead of data values, are being rendered by the thematic presentation. To prepare your data, go to the **Views** menu and click **View Variables**. Select **J&J Video Option1%Mkt Share** as the layer variable to be displayed.

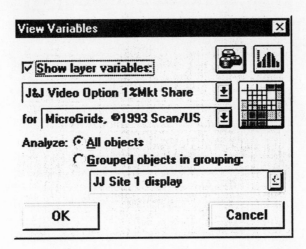

To open the dialog box shown below, click the "Strata Manager" button: [icon]. Click the presentation icon next to the desired stratum, and a window shade will replace the color icon for the stratum (i.e., a hidden stratum has been created).

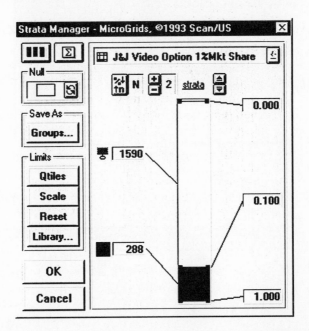

Click on **Groups** button and save your data as a new grouping.

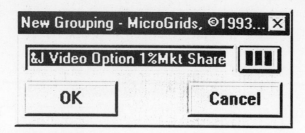

Click **OK** (on several open windows). Next, from the **Data** menu, click **Copy Data** and copy the data to the Windows clipboard for **Objects in groups**.

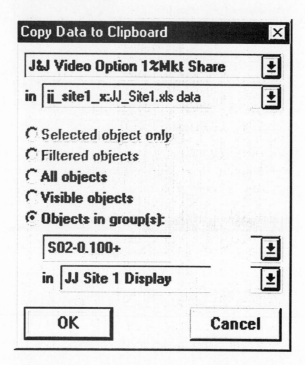

Click **OK**. Now open Excel and paste the data into a spreadsheet (use the Windows copy command or the key combination Ctrl+V).

	1	2	3	4	5	6	7	8	
1	[data]	288	1	1	1	jj_site1_x:	1	1	
2	Key	Group	Name	huffprob9:J&J Video Option 1%Mkt Share					
3	#33111/17:		2 Grid 33111	0.10811					
4	#33111/17:		2 Grid 33111	0.12628					
5	#33111/17:		2 Grid 33111	0.12173					
6	#33111/17:		2 Grid 33111	0.13041					
7	#33111/17:		2 Grid 33111	0.13349					
8	#33111/17:		2 Grid 33111	0.11403					
9	#33111/17:		2 Grid 33111	0.12373					
10	#33111/18:		2 Grid 33111	0.13015					
11	#33111/18:		2 Grid 33111	0.14965					
12	#33111/18:		2 Grid 33111	0.14274					
13	#33111/18:		2 Grid 33111	0.13684					

Exporting Scan/US demographic data: As an example, we will copy the "Average annual expenditure per household for videos, tapes, disks" variable from the Home Electronics datalist and the "Total

Households (hh90)" variable from the data in the BasePak and paste the data into the spreadsheet shown above.

For these tasks, the relevant data need to be available to the consumer layer. Several data lists can be loaded onto a layer (although only one can be active at a time). In this example, we use information from the Scan/US data lists on home electronics and key demographics, as well as the probability estimates from the gravity model. To load the home electronics data list, go to the **Data** menu in the Scan/US program, choose **Data Center,** select **'93 Home Electronics**, and click the **Load** button (if the data is not already loaded).

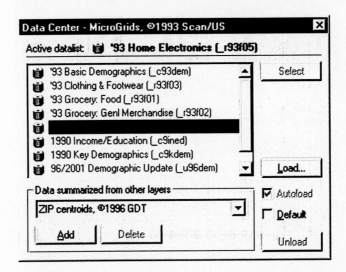

Next, go to the **Data** menu and click **Copy Data.** Choose Home Electronics as your database in the drop down menu and select the variables that you want to copy into your spreadsheet. In this example, restrict the demographic data to be copied to the strata group that you specified earlier (e.g., J&J Video Option1%Mkt Share) or simply choose **Filtered Objects**. This ensures that only data for the microgrids that obtained choice probability values of more than 10 percent for J&J Video Option 1 will be copied.

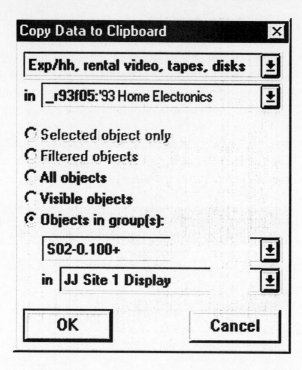

Go back to Excel and paste the data into the spreadsheet, making sure that the data are copied beginning with the correct row (i.e., matched on key # given in column 1).

Similarly, copy the Total Households variable from the data in your BasePak, and paste the data into the spreadsheet.

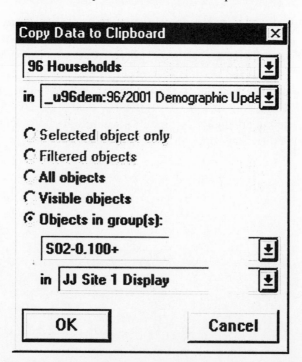

Now you can create variables that combine demographic information and choice probabilities from the gravity model. To compute potential sales for J&J Video Option 1 for the "filtered" area (assuming that this is the primary trade area), multiply the column containing the probability values (the variable is called huffprob9 on the spreadsheet) by the Total Households and by Average Annual Expenditure per Household for Video rentals, disks, and tapes. You can then total the potential sales across MicroGrids to derive an estimate for the total potential sales for the retail site under consideration.

Prepare your own Excel data for import into Scan/US

When preparing your own Excel data for input to Scan/US, you need to ensure that your Excel data file meets the following specifications to make it readable by the Scan/US software:

- Put your object keys in column A. An object key is a unique identifier for each record that matches the data with the geographic object to which it pertains. These keys must be in text format. A pound sign (#) in front of numeric keys makes them "text." (For best performance, sort the object keys in ascending order.)
- Your data columns must have column headings without any numbers in their names.
- You must define a named range called "**database**" that includes all the cells containing the column names, object keys, and data. You must complete this step, or Scan/US may not read your data correctly. If you modify the number of rows and columns in your data file, you must redefine the range of "**database**".

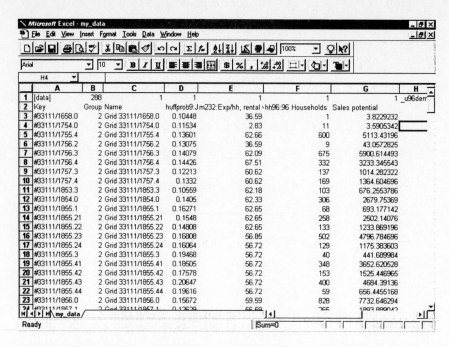

■ You must save your spreadsheet in Excel 4.0 format. For convenience, save it in the Scanus\userdata folder. Close the file before trying to import it into Scan/US.

Display imported data within Scan/US

Now you can load your data into Scan/US, more specifically, to the layer that contains your objects codes. In this example, make sure that MicroGrids is the active layer. Next, go to the **Data** menu and choose **Load Data** and select the file you saved. You may then create thematic views to visualize your data and conduct further analyses.

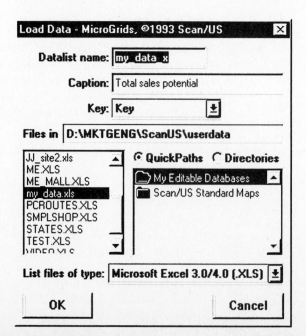

Glossary

Data: Scan/US provides census-based demographic data with most geographic features in the BasePak. Data are automatically loaded with each feature in a study area.

Groups: By creating groups, you can classify objects on a layer into distinct and unique subsets. In general, you can select any group to operate on as a unit. For instance, you can copy, paste, hide, or show groups on a layer.

A classification of objects into groups is called a grouping. A grouping can consist of a number of groups. Because objects can be classified in any number of ways, you can define any number of groupings on the layer. You can create as many groupings as you like, limited only by the amount of memory on your computer. However, only one grouping can be active at a time on any given layer.

Grouping objects is a powerful feature in Scan/US. As a fundamental tool for handling multiple objects, grouping is a first step in analyzing a territory, or in limiting an analysis to a specific region. For example, you can examine sales across territories by creating a group for each territory, such as California, Washington, and Oregon in the western region/group, and then look at the group's data in "QuickLook."

Layers: Geographic features, such as states, counties, roads, or geology, are loaded as layers into the study area, each feature on its own layer. In the gravity model application, there are special names for two of those layers: the consumer layer and the location layer. The *consumer layer* contains (demographic) geo-coded information about your clientele -- at the level of detail needed for your analysis (e.g., mostly data provided by Scan/US such as MicroGrids or block-level census data). The *location layer* contains information about the location of the sites that you wish to consider in your analysis.

Each item of a feature on a layer is called an *object*. For example, California is an object on the Places 500T+ layer. Although several features or layers are present in a study area, only one layer can be active at a time. The terms *feature* and *layer* are often used interchangeably.

Object: A set of points, lines, or polygons in a spatial database that represent a real-world entity.

Object key: An object key is a unique identifier for each record. This key matches the data with the geographic object to which it pertains. You have object keys that match your data to standard geographical units, such as zip codes or census tracts. Or you can have your own unique keys that identify your store or branch office locations.

References

Scan/US Basic Skills, fourth edition, June 1996.
4Scan/US User's Guide, first edition, December 1994.

J&J FAMILY VIDEO CASE[*]

Jack and Jerilyn Rodeman are longtime residents of Scottsdale, Arizona. Jack recently took early retirement from the aviation division of a leading firm in electronic instrumentation and controls after several years of successfully managing its manufacturing operations. Jeri is currently working part-time as an independent software consultant to small businesses in the Phoenix area. As Jack and Jeri planned the next phase of their life, they decided to open a small service business, such as a cybercafe, a restaurant, or a video store. After discussions with their children and friends, they decided to explore the feasibility of opening a video store close to their home.

Over 85 percent of U.S. households have a VCR and about 50 percent of American households rent a video at least once a month. A "VCR household" had an average of 47 rentals per year at an average price of $2.50 per rental. In 1996, video rentals and sales were estimated to be around $18 billion, with rentals representing about half the industry revenues, and the rest attributed to sales of used video tapes (at around $10 per tape) and other related products. Nationally, there were about 27,500 video stores, but this number had declined from a high of 31,500 in 1990. Although some industry observers believed further consolidation would lead to fewer video stores, others, like Bob Finlayson of the Video Software Dealers Association, believed that consumers will drive only a short distance (three or four miles) to rent a video rental, and that the number of video outlets would actually increase over the next few years. In fact, a recent trend has been the growth of video rental and sales through supermarkets ($1.9 billion in 1996), mass merchandisers such as K-Mart ($200 million in 1996), and even gasoline stations.

Industry leader, Blockbuster Entertainment Group, operated 14 percent of all stores and had an over 20 percent share of the revenues. Other large companies included Portland-based Hollywood Entertainment and Philadelphia-based West-Coast Entertainment. Blockbuster competed by offering consumers a large selection with an emphasis on recent releases, with stores carrying over 40 copies of some new releases. Blockbuster had a number of large stores that were over 6000 square feet in size, and had over 20,000 rental units under 5000 or more titles. Smaller video stores were typically less than 2000 square feet and carried fewer than 6000 rental units. Video rental prices varied greatly with new releases, renting for about $3.50 for two nights at Blockbuster and $3 for a single night at Hollywood Entertainment. Older movies rented for about $1.50 to $2.00 for three nights, and "family movies" rented for as little as 99 cents for two nights. Video stores often had ongoing promotions, such as half-price rentals during "happy hours" (e.g., 9 am to 10 am), or special pricing on selected days (e.g., Tuesdays), and senior citizens discounts.

---

[*] This exercise describes a hypothetical situation. It was developed by Arvind Rangaswamy and Katrin Starke using publicly available information.

Jack and Jeri determined that site location would be the primary factor that determined the competitive environment the new store would face and therefore its long-term viability. They hired a consultant friend, Ruby Jackson, to do preliminary research to assess the competitive environment in the catchment area within which they planned to locate their new store. Based on her experience, Ms. Jackson concluded that several factors influence what video stores consumers patronize: (1) the distance of the store from their homes, and (2) overall attractiveness of each store, which could depend on such factors as proximity to other shops, variety of videos for rent, service quality, average price, and size of the store. She identified eight existing stores with which the proposed new store would compete in the geographical area of interest and gathered preliminary information about these stores. She organized the information into the following table:

Store	Proximity to Other General Shops (1 poor to 7 good)	Estimated Number of Titles Carried	Service Quality (1 good to 7 excellent)	Estimated Average price per Rental	Size (square feet)	Estimated Percent Unit Market Share in Study Area (from traffic counts)
Discovery Video	2	2,000	6	1.95	1,200	5
Blockbuster Entertainment	6	4,000	3	2.30	4,400	25
Video Connection	2	800	6	1.70	1,000	5
Video Power	5	2,500	4	2.10	1,800	12
Hollywood Entertainment	3	3,500	5	2.20	3,000	20
Movie Arcade	7	1,500	5	1.75	1,000	10
Local Supermarket	7	300	1	2.40	200	5
Action Video	2	1,300	7	2.85	1,400	18

While Blockbuster and Hollywood offered wide variety, such stores as Action Video focused on the latest releases, adult video, and suspense and adventure titles. Video Connection and Movie Arcade focused on older movies and "seconds" of recent releases. Ruby guessed the combined annual sales of these video stores to be around $8 million per year (including sales to people outside the study area).

Jack and Jeri wanted their video store to carry only family-oriented and children's videos (PG or G ratings). They planned to carry a maximum of 1600 titles, including new releases, and they hoped to realize an average rental rate of $2.10. Jeri had access to a software program called Scan/US, which she used in her work helping small businesses to develop direct marketing programs. She decided to use this software to evaluate three alternative sites where space was currently available. The table below shows the characteristics of these sites:

Location	Proximity to Other General Shops (1 poor to 7 good)	Estimated Number of Titles	Service Quality (1 good to 7 excellent)	Estimated Average Price Per Rental	Size (square feet)
Option 1	2	1,200	6	2.10	1,200
Option 2	4	1,600	5	2.10	2,500
Option 3	3	1,200	6	2.10	1,200

EXERCISES

1. Using the tabular data, develop and justify an overall measure of store attractiveness for each existing store and for the three potential sites.

    To answer the following questions, you will need to build a gravity model using Scan/US and Microsoft Excel. Select **J&J Video and Competitors** as your location layer.

2. Insert the overall index of store attractiveness for each store into the gravity model and evaluate which of the three locations that Jack and Jeri are considering would achieve the highest market share. (To evaluate one site at a time, choose a store attractiveness index value of zero for sites not under consideration.)

3. Jeri estimated that the total annual operating costs of an established video store would be roughly $300,000 for a 1200 square-foot store and about $450,000 for a 2500 square-foot store at all three locations. She also estimated that the cost of opening a new store would be between $250,000 and $300,000, depending on its size. These initial costs cover purchasing such items as tapes, furniture and fittings, and computer equipment and software. Are any of the proposed store locations a good business proposition given this cost structure? Why or why not?

4. Jack and Jeri are also concerned about the long-term viability of video stores in view of the growth of direct TV broadcasts and the expansion of cable offerings. They wondered whether the gravity model could be modified in some way to take into account the potential threats posed by these developments.

Chapter 7

TUTORIAL FOR PROMOTIONAL SPENDING ANALYSIS (MASSMART)

Concept

The Promotional Spending Analysis model is based on a model developed by Tellis and Zufryden (1995). The model is designed to help retailers to maximize their cumulative profits over a planning horizon by deciding which brands to promote and the price discounts to offer on each brand.

At the heart of this retailer model is a customer response function:

$$E(S_{ijt}) = E(Q_{ijt} \mid B, C, V) \, P_{ijt} \, (B \mid C, V) \, P_{it} \, (C \mid V) \qquad (1)$$

where

$$
\begin{aligned}
i &= \text{customer,} \\
j &= \text{brand,} \\
t &= \text{time period,} \\
E(S) &= \text{expected sales,} \\
V &= \text{store visit,} \\
C &= \text{category purchase,} \\
B &= \text{brand choice,} \\
Q &= \text{quantity purchases, and} \\
P &= \text{purchase probability.}
\end{aligned}
$$

The model in equation (1) has three sub-models: a purchase-quantity model, a brand-choice model, and a purchase-incidence model.

The customer's decision process is represented as a (nested) logit model where the purchase incidence is represented by a binary logit model (purchase or not) and the brand choice is represented by a multinomial logit model. The probability that customer i will make a purchase in the product category during period *t given* a store visit is

$$P_{it}(C \mid V) = \frac{1}{1 + \exp[-b_0 + b_1 \text{CatPur}_i + b_2 \text{Inv}_{it} + b_3 \text{Inc}_{it})]}, \qquad (2)$$

where

$CatPur_i$ = mean long-term probability that the customer purchases in the product category,

Inc_{it} = category attractiveness index (log of the denominator of equation (3)),

Inv_{it} = number of units of inventory the customer held at the start of period t, and

$b_0..b_3$ = model coefficients to be estimated.

They model brand choice as a multinomial logit model (conditional on category purchase in a period) as

$$P_{ijt}(B|C) = \frac{\exp(\beta X_{ijt} + \gamma_j \text{Disc}_{ijt})}{\sum_k \exp(\beta X_{ikt} + \gamma_k \text{Disc}_{ikt})}, \tag{3}$$

where

$Disc_{ijt}$ = discount level available to customer i for brand j in period t;

X_{ijt} = vector of causal variables, including brand loyalty, indicator of previous brand chosen, list price, feature indicator, display indicator;

γ_j = parameter for discount for brand j, to be estimated;

β = vector of causal parameters ($= \beta_0, \beta_1, ...\beta_v$), to be estimated; and

k = index for brands in the choice set.

Finally, they model the expected quantity of brand j purchased by customer i during time period t *given* that the customer chooses brand j as

$$E(Q_{ijt}|B) = \exp(a_0 + a_1 \text{Price}_{ijt} + a_{2j} \text{Disc}_{ijt} + a_3 \text{Inv}_{it} + a_4 H_{ijt}),$$

where

E = expectation operator,

$Price_{ijt}$ = list price for brand j at time t,

Disc_{ijt} =   discount for the specific brand,

Inv_{it} =   inventory of that category of household product at beginning of period t, and

H_{ijt} =   brand attractiveness = $\beta X_{ijt} + \gamma_j \text{Disc}_{ijt}$ for each brand j

$a_0, \ldots a_4$ =   model coefficients to be estimated.

H accounts for why customers buy different quantities of different brands; for example, a customer might buy a small amount of (expensive) premium coffee for guests and a larger quantity of less expensive coffee for everyday use.

Software

Promotional Spending Analysis helps retailers to develop brand-promotion schemes that will maximize a retail outlet's profits. This spreadsheet exercise implements the promotional analysis model for MassMart, Inc., a big mass merchandiser. Your task is to analyze and improve the promotional activities of the company's store in State College, Pennsylvania. The software includes three models for analyzing the store's promotional activities: the Choice Model, the Quantity Model and the Promotion Model.

NOTE: *The Promotional Spending Analysis Excel spreadsheet relies on the Analysis Toolpak add-in to run a regression analysis. If this add-in is not already loaded, you should load it manually. To do so, go to the* **Tools** *menu, then* **Add-Ins**, *and choose* **Analysis ToolPak**. *If this option is not in the list, you will have to install it via the setup program in Excel (or MS Office).*

From the **Model** menu select **Promotional Spending Analysis** (Promote.xls) to see the **Introduction**.

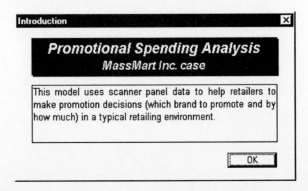

From the **Model** menu of the Excel spreadsheet, choose **Main Menu**. The **Main Menu** dialog box looks like this:

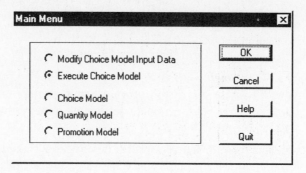

Choice model

From the **Main Menu** dialog box select **Execute Choice Model** and click **OK**. The Choice Model uses information on the quantity of various brands purchased by consumers and on retailer promotion activities at the time of purchase, such as discounts, feature ads, and displays. The model assesses the likelihood that a consumer will choose a particular brand based on the promotional activities directed at all the brands. After the model executes it will display a spreadsheet that includes coefficients of each variable and the associated asymptotic t-statistics. The coefficient of each variable indicates the magnitude of that variable's impact on a consumer's probability of choosing each brand. The t-statistics indicate the statistical significance of the coefficients.

The Choice Model output screen looks like this :

PROMOTIONAL SPENDING ANALYSIS
Which and How Much?

Case Name: MassMart

| Choice Model | | | | Coefficients | 8.0 | -3.1 | 8.9 | 1.4 | 1.4 | 0.0 | 0.0 | -0.4 |
| | | | | T stats | 3.9 | -2.3 | 3.7 | 2.6 | 2.3 | 0.1 | 0.0 | -0.5 |

Customer	Month	Brands	Quantity	Choice	Loyalty	List Price	Discount	Display	Feature	Wisk	All	Tide
1	1	Wisk	0	0	0.07	3.25	0.63	0	0	1	0	0
		All	0	0	0.07	3.10	0.71	0	0	0	1	0
		Tide	1	1	0.80	3.30	0.82	1	1	0	0	1
		Yes	0	0	0.07	2.95	0.86	0	0	0	0	0
	2	Wisk	0	0	0.05	3.25	0.63	0	0	1	0	0
		All	0	0	0.05	3.10	0.71	0	0	0	1	0
		Tide	0	0	0.64	3.67	0.82	0	0	0	0	1
		Yes	1	1	0.25	2.95	0.60	0	1	0	0	0
	3	Wisk	0	0	0.04	3.32	0.12	0	0	1	0	0
		All	0	0	0.04	3.05	0.33	0	0	0	1	0
		Tide	0	0	0.51	3.55	0.12	0	0	0	0	1

Quantity model

From the **Model** menu, select **Main Menu** to get the **Main Menu** dialog box. Select **Quantity Model** and click **OK** to see the Quantity Model output.

NOTE: *Sometimes when **Quantity Model** is chosen from the **Main Menu** dialog box, Excel displays an error message, either **Analysis Toolpak Absent** or **Add-in Absent**. In this case you need to install the Analysis Toolpak: from the **Tools** menu, select **Add-Ins**. Excel will display the **Add-Ins** dialog box. Check **Analysis Toolpak**. The program will then be able to run the **Quantity Model**.*

The Quantity Model uses the Choice Model's output as its input. It uses the quantity of the product each consumer consumed and the retailer's promotional activities as its inputs. The Quantity Model calculates the responsiveness of the quantity each consumer consumes as a function of several variables (e.g., regular list price and excess inventory at the consumer's home).

The Quantity Model output looks like this:

Promotion model

Using the Promotion Model, you can develop recommendations for the promotional activities of a retail outlet. It allows you to:

- Select the brands for which it is profitable to run promotional activities, and

■   Select the ideal promotional vehicles (discount, displays, or features) for each brand.

From the **Model** menu, select **Main Menu** to see the **Main Menu** dialog box. Select **Promotion Model**. Click **OK**. The Promotion Model's analysis area will be displayed:

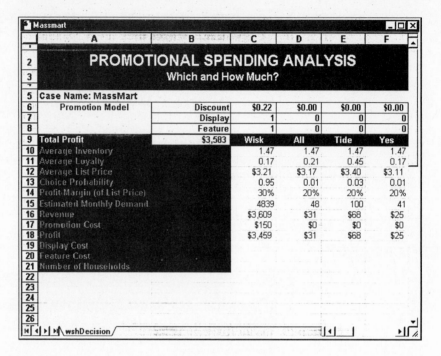

You can use Excel's Solver tool to select a set of promotional activities to maximize Total Profit.

1.   From the **Tools** menu, select **Solver** to see the **Solver Parameters** dialog box, which looks like this:

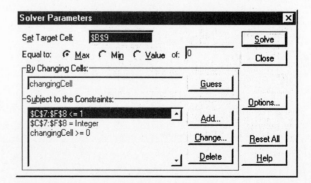

2.   In the **Set Target Cell** area, enter the cell number that contains the Total Profit amount (e.g., $B$9).

3.   In the **By Changing Cells** area, enter the range of cells that contain the amount of discount and the display and feature variables (e.g., $C$6:$F$8).

4. In the **Subject to Constraints** area, enter constraints that ensure that

    a. the display and feature variables are equal to either 1 or 0,
    b. the discount amounts are greater than or equal to 0.

        The following equations are just one way of achieving the above constraints:

        $C$7:$F$8 < =   1
        $C$7:$F$8   =   Integer
        $C$6:$F$8 > =   0.

5. Click **Solve**. The Promotion Model displays the optimal promotional activities to maximize the retailer's total profit.

6. Use Solver in a similar manner to answer the questions at the end of the MassMart case.

Reference

Tellis, J. Gerard and Zufryden, Fred S. 1995, "Tackling the Retailer Decision Maze: Which Brands to Discount, How Much, When and Why?" *Marketing Science*, Vol. 14, No. 3, pp. 271-299.

MASSMART INC. CASE*

It was Friday, February 23, 1997. Donna Sullivan, marketing manager for MassMart for the central Pennsylvania region, was in her office. She was writing a report to her boss, Jack Chen, vice president of marketing for the company. In January, Jack had asked her to do a preliminary strategic review of the company's promotion programs for its store in State College, Pennsylvania. MassMart is a leading mass merchandiser with over 80 stores in Pennsylvania, Ohio, and Maryland. The company has had a strong presence in central Pennsylvania for over 25 years. Competition has, however, increased recently with two Wal-Mart stores and one Sam's Club outlet established in State College in the last five years.

In preparing her report, Donna spent one morning at the local university library reading articles about in-store sales promotions. One article (by Gerard Tellis and Fred Zufryden in *Marketing Science*) in particular caught her eye. The authors described how to plan sales promotions in retail stores using scanner-panel data (individual-level purchase data collected by the scanner at the checkout counter). Using these data, analysts can track the purchases made by a selected sample of consumers. She knew that the State College MassMart collected this kind of data and used these data to identify trends and plan inventory.

The ideas in the article impressed her because they suggested an approach that was different from what her company had been doing. She became increasingly skeptical about the current promotion strategy and excited by the prospect of developing a new promotion strategy.

Background

MassMart established its store in downtown State College in 1975. It was first mass merchandiser in State College, a college town that is the home of Penn State University. The company had established relationships with several wholesalers and brokers on the East coast from whom it purchased products for sale to local residents and students. Between 1984 and 1994, as the university and the town expanded, sales at Mass-Mart had grown over 500 percent. Its main competitors during this decade were a Sears and a J.C. Penney store located in a mall a few miles out of town. However, in the past two years, there had been increasing pressure on sales from the two Wal-Marts and the Sam's Club, also located a few miles from the town center.

Donna thought that the past increases in sales at the MassMart store in State College were in large part caused by the company's promotional policy of always passing on the trade discounts it received from wholesalers to its consumers. The logic behind this policy was simple: those

---

* This case was developed by Jianan Wu under the guidance of Professor Arvind Rangaswamy. The case describes a hypothetical situation.

discounts caused no incremental costs to MassMart but helped attract new consumers from nearby communities, some of whom would keep coming back to buy other merchandise, thereby contributing to growth in sales and profits.

When Donna met with Jack in January to review 1996's promotional activities, both thought that they needed some fresh ideas for a more intelligent strategy for promoting sales. The tougher competition had led to thinner profit margins and anything they could do to increase profitability would help them compete better.

Scanner-panel data

MassMart had installed an optical scanner system in its State College store in 1988, with the primary objective of improving checkout service and the store's accounting and inventory systems. This investment paid off: The store inventory was better monitored than ever before; price changes have been easier to implement; and check out time decreased by an average of 40 percent. To keep better track of consumer needs and trends, MassMart developed its own "scanner panel," consisting of a representative sample of consumers from the shopping areas of its key stores. Panel members get a five percent discount for shopping at MassMart when they show their membership cards at checkout. Data on their purchases go into a database maintained by the company. Separately MassMart also kept records on prices, in-store promotions, special store displays, and newspaper inserts featuring specials at these stores. The complete scanner-panel database could provide all of the following data:

- The regular prices of all brands at the time of purchase
- The identification numbers of the panel members (to protect their privacy, the company did not store members' names directly in the database)
- The dates on which each panel member made purchases
- The product category and brands purchased
- The quantity of each item purchased
- Temporary price cuts (if any) for all the brands in a category at the time of purchase
- Whether each item purchased was part of an in-store display
- Whether each item purchased was featured in the local newspaper

(Exhibit 1 shows a sample of scanner-panel data for the liquid-laundry-detergent product category.)

Donna talked to Jack Chen about some of the ideas she had for using scanner data in planning promotions: "Jack, I think we should revamp our promotion program. The more I think about our current promotion strategy, the more I am convinced that we need to do something very different. You know, we simply pass on trade deals directly to consumers, but we have never looked at whether this is a good strategy. These trade deals are designed by our wholesalers and the packaged-goods companies. I am not sure these discounts really serve our interests here in State College. We really have no idea what discount levels would increase our sales and profitability most."

"Donna, I guess you're right. Go on."

"We often give discounts on several brands at the same time just because we have gotten trade discounts on all of them. Our sales for all the discounted brands increase, but I wonder whether this makes sense. It might be better sometimes to combine what we get in trade deals so that we can give a larger discount on the brand Wal-Mart is promoting. Loyal consumers of the nondiscounted brands will still buy that brand."

"But Donna, won't our profits go down if we discount just the brand Wal-Mart discounts?"

"Not necessarily! According to an article I read, when two brands are on discount fewer people switch brands than when only one is discounted. If we discount both brands our opportunity costs are higher. Loyal consumers of both brands who would purchase the brand anyway without a discount are just subsidized by the discount. Of course the opportunity costs depend on the number of loyal consumers of each brand. But I think offering simultaneous discounts on two brands is likely to be less profitable than discounting just one brand."

"Donna, I think you have something. But we often get trade deals simultaneously for several brands from our wholesalers. How would we know which brand to discount and how much to discount?"

"To figure that out, I think we need to look at our promotions from the point of view of our consumers. That article I read said that the key is to understand consumer responses to price-cuts, displays, and features. Response will of course vary for different brands and product categories. I think looking at our scanner-panel data may give us some insights."

"Donna, if the best discounts to offer vary by brand and category, won't we have to continuously monitor the effectiveness of our promotions and the promotions of other stores and change our discounts to suit each specific situation? If so, won't we need to use this database on an ongoing basis? All this seems so much more complicated than the simple policy we have now."

"It is! But we already have the data. The MIS department told me that it wouldn't be hard to put together a database, at least as an experiment for one or two categories. In fact, they got us some data on the liquid-detergent category last week. I also got some software from a professor in the business school so that we can build a computer model to evaluate promotion effectiveness. Let me try it out with the detergent category, and we can take it from there."

"Good idea, Donna! Let me know what you find out. I don't want to do anything new without testing it out carefully. I am also concerned about whether managers at our 79 other stores, who are not fans of all this computer stuff, will adopt your approach. What we have now is so easy for them to follow."

"I know, but easier may not be better."

The promotion model

The software Donna got from her professor friend builds a choice model of consumers using the scanner-panel data and a profit model for the retailer that is based on the consumer-choice model. Together the two models incorporate three components:

Consumer-brand-choice component: This component assesses the probability (P) that consumers will purchase a specific brand in response to retail promotion variables, such as price discount, in-store display, and newspaper feature. The model captures consumers' loyalty to certain brands through a loyalty index that it derives from panel members' histories of past purchases of alternative brands.

Purchase-quantity component: This component of the model determines how many units of a brand a consumer will purchase once he or she decides to buy a particular brand. The quantity purchased (Q) will depend on the price cut, the consumer's current inventory of that product category, and the consumption rate of the product. The model estimates household inventory and consumption rates by examining the panel member's past purchase history.

Retailer-promotion component: The third component of the model computes retailer profits based on the brand discounted and the size of the discount. The retailer's profit function is constructed as follows:

$$Profit = \sum\ profit\ margin \times P \times Q$$

where *P* and *Q* together provide an estimate of the demand for a brand in a period, and the summation is over all the brands in the category. The model assumes that the retailer seeks an optimal promotion scheme to maximize profits over a planning period.

Although MassMart carries 11 brands of liquid laundry detergent, the four most popular brands are Tide, Wisk, All, and Yes, which account for more than 80 percent of the sales in the category. Donna decided to use these four brands to conduct her experiment.

With all this preliminary work behind her, Donna Sullivan pulled up this new software and began her analysis.

Customer ID	Date	Brand Purchased	Quantity	Regular Price	Discount	Display	Feature
1001	03/01/95	Tide	50 Oz	$ 3.55	$ 0.43	No	No
1001	03/29/95	Tide	64 Oz	$ 3.99	$ 0.54	Yes	Yes
1001	04/25/95	Tide	50 Oz	$ 3.55	$ 0.45	No	No
1001	05/28/95	All	50 Oz	$ 2.99	$ 0.50	Yes	No
1001	06/27/95	Tide	50 Oz	$ 3.60	$ 0.45	No	No
1001	07/22/95	Tide	50 Oz	$ 3.60	$ 0.20	No	No
1001	08/29/95	All	64 Oz	$ 3.15	$ 0.60	Yes	Yes
1001	09/24/95	Tide	50 Oz	$ 3.65	$ 0.42	No	No
1001	10/28/95	All	100 Oz	$ 4.99	$ 1.00	Yes	Yes
1001	11/25/95	Tide	50 Oz	$ 3.99	$ 0.50	No	No

EXHIBIT 1

A segment of the scanner-panel database for liquid laundry detergent shows the purchases made by a single individual over 10 periods along with the store-environment information (e.g., regular price, display) at the time of purchase.

EXERCISES

NOTE: This exercise is based on a small data set to facilitate analysis in Excel. It consists of data for eight consumers over 10 periods in which they choose from four brands (providing a total of 320 data points).

1. Summarize the important factors that influence consumer brand choice within the detergent category. If a consumer chooses a particular brand, what other factors will influence the quantity that consumer will purchase?

2. Based on the sample input data, what is the best promotion strategy? Explain why you think that strategy will work. For the promotion strategy that you recommend, what will be the composition of sales? What proportion of sales comes from brand switchers, and what proportion comes from consumers stocking up (i.e., purchase acceleration)?

3. Does promoting two brands simultaneously make sense? Why or why not?

4. How do the trade deals (profit margins) affect retailers' promotion decisions (which brand and how much)? Should trade deals always be passed on to the store consumers? Why or why not?

5. Should Jack Chen adopt this approach for all MassMart stores? Why or why not?

INDEX